Praise for *Emergence: A Path to Presence...*

"This is a delightful guide to expanding one's definition of intelligence to include the wonderfully insightful powers of our hearts and bodies. Emergence is a welcomed perspective on creating a world that works for everyone through the essential work of personal transformation."

~MICHAEL L. PENN, JR., MD, PhD,
Managing Director,
Health Equity Ventures

"S'Marie Young has written a captivating book about her journey of awakening and has managed to make — through her engaging writing style and ability to tell her story — that which is personal into something beautifully universal."

~GINGER LAPID-BOGDA PhD,
author of *What Type of Leader Are You?*
Using the Enneagram System to Identify and Grow Your Leadership Strengths and Achieve Maximum Success

"With fluid prose and great courage, the author nudges readers step-by-step towards their own personal/spiritual emergence by sharing her own pilgrimage and gradual awakening to authenticity. Her exquisite poems, which punctuate important milestones in the book, profoundly tap into inner depths of knowing that would otherwise be truly ineffable."

~LIANA BECKETT
Licensed Marriage and Family Therapist
Psychotherapist and co-author of *Leaving the Enchanted Forest* (Harper Collins).

"S'Marie Young has told a compelling narrative that brings together her journey into meditation and the powerful concepts of the head, heart and body intelligence from the Enneagram. Emergence: A Path to Presence *weaves together her own personal story of discovery and the experience of essence with knowledge from the Enneagram and the wisdom traditions."*

~DENISE DANIELS, PhD,
Enneagram Teacher/Author and daughter
of David N. Daniels, M.D. one of the
founding fathers of today's Enneagram

"This beautiful mix of stories, evocative poetry and guided exploration invites us to expand our awareness and explore our humanity. S'Marie Young invites us into a rich personal journey of self discovery, it is an invitation well worth saying 'Yes!' to."

~CYNTHIA LOY DARST, MCC,
Author of Meet Your Inside Team: How to
Turn Internal Conflict into Clarity and Move
Forward with Your Life

*"*Emergence *is compelling—I couldn't put it down. I've not come across the depth of understanding and clarity that S'Marie Young has writing about her own journey of awakening. Her vast wisdom and experience spoke to my heart at deep levels, in a way that is both refreshing and unique. I'm ready for a big change in my life and this book resonated at exactly the right time."*

~SHERYL ROUSH,
International Speaker and author
of Heart of a Woman in Business.

"We all know that 'the unexamined life is not worth living,' but few of us are willing to go through the process of examining our own life in all its unpleasant (and pleasant) detail; fewer still are willing to bring the best aspects of modern psychological and spiritual wisdom to the task; even fewer are willing to share the results of that inquiry with the world. S'Marie Young has done all that, in a deeply revealing and ultimately uplifting memoir."

~Jerry Yudelson,
Author of *The Godfather of Green:*
An Eco-Spiritual Memoir

"The author takes us through a powerful journey and coming of age through captivating life stories, soul searching, and heartfelt poetry, with just the right amount of spice and naughtiness. She leads the reader to transform from the inside out and recommends tools to achieve greater consciousness, awareness, empowerment and inner connection! S'Marie's poems took me to another place and time and brought her message full-circle about the importance of being expressive and standing in our truth."

~Janet Andrews,
CEO, Executive Career Coach,
A Career Above

"One thing I love about S'Marie is her introspective self-expression, which is vulnerable, honest and clear. In her new book, Emergence, she's embodied that transparency while walking through her own journey. Her stories are raw and relatable, all while showing readers how she moved from one step to the next, as we all do: from the way we are formed, to self-awareness, to becoming who we are now, to finally becoming who we are meant to be—from experience to growth to purpose.

Thoughtful and inspiring, her stories will have you nodding along in understanding. She has a way of leading the reader along on her journey while providing tips and tools to help you on yours. I especially resonated with her younger years, of a joyful soul squashed down and misunderstood, only to be found once again, years later. Thought-provoking and insightful, this is must-read."

~JANA BEAMAN,
Certified Master Coach Trainer

"A beautiful and powerful account of S'Marie Young's personal journey to rediscover and reinforce the harmony and alignment between her heart, body, and mind. How do we react when things don't go our way? What internal narratives do we adopt that shape and define our experiences? How do we quiet the noise and identify our true inner, authentic voice? These are some of the thought provoking questions and expressions S'Marie explores in Emergence through prose and poetry. It›s a brave and inspiring self-inquiry with practical and accessible information on achieving presence, with lessons for improving our relationships, leadership, and connections to the world around us."

~TONY GOTTSCHALK,
Biotechnology Industry Senior Executive

"S'Marie's honest account of her life's journey, leading her to know her true Self, is inspiring, and made me want to look more closely at my journey. Her stories and experiences inspire the reader to reflect on one's own inner journey, and to discover the gifts along the way in our stories, and our healing. I enjoyed her clarity of writing, and her accessibility to wisdom and insight. Thank you S'Marie! I highly recommend this book to those of us searching to know the truth."

~CAROL HYDE,
Licensed Marriage and Family Therapist

"Emergence *is an honest and courageous examination of the author's life that represents the transformative power of bringing to light our personal and collective history. S'Marie's experiences serve to unite us and reignite our own souls' journey. This book is both an inspiration and a guide for those who want to journey within and come into deeper contact with themselves. I was touched by the universality of the stories of personal evolution, and the courage it takes to bring them forward."*

~Diana Redmond,
Senior Faculty and Partner of
Deep Coaching Institute

"This is a deeply insightful, clear, and extremely enjoyable exploration of the path into presence. You are holding a truly gorgeous book from an author who I am blessed to have journeyed beside for a time. S'Marie's poetry, heart and clarity of wisdom gleaned from deep study and intimate experience illumines a path of transformation that is truly stunning. I particularly value the practical action steps which guide our own personal passage, unfolding a presence filled life. I highly recommend for any conscious leader journeying toward joy, fulfillment and impact. Thank you S'Marie for this brave gift so many courageous years in the making."

~JEANEEN R. SCHMIDT, PCC, CPCC,
Leadership Coach and Consultant

"S'Marie weaves her own deeply personal stories and poetry with wisdom from the Enneagram, neuroscience, spiritual traditions and contemporary psychology, providing an accessible and relevant guide that supports a life of learning and emergence. Speaking from the heart, S'Marie guides the reader in their own self-discovery while providing questions, guidance, and candid self-revelations that are as relatable as they are inspiring."

~SUSAN PENN,
Founder, Embold Coaching
& Consulting, Inc.

"The authors honest retelling of her own life journey, combined with the pointers to the reader, make for a breath of centered air that guide you to be your own best and complete person"

~GREG SALOMON,
Executive Vice President
Primary Funding

"Emergence is a rich journey of deep discovery and abundant self love, told through the honest lens of the feminine. S'Marie weaves an experiential tapestry of soul wisdom, creativity, high intellect and practical "head, heart, and body" solutions to becoming your truest self."

~JANUARY SUAREZ, DC
Chiropractor and Energy Healer

"We all have our history, our stories and events that mold who we think we are. In reading this book you take a journey with S'Marie. Wherever you may be in your life with family, career, or relationships; the questions that she asks the reader to consider are meant to nudge you to a deeper level. They provide a structure and platform to guide, bring focus; and ultimately to align you to your own truth. She does this with heart and compassion."

~PAULA WEST, MD

EMERGENCE

A PATH *to* PRESENCE

EMERGENCE
A PATH *to* PRESENCE

Discovering Your True Inner Self
for a More Fulfilled Life

S'Marie Young

Book and cover design and production: Beth Fountain, Fountain Ink.
Printed in United States of America
First edition 2021

Library of Congress Control Number: 2021910094

ISBN 978-1-7357830-0-0

Published by

S'MARIE
YOUNG

Cover: detail from *Birds*, by Franz Marc, Wikimedia Commons (PD-US-expired)

Dedication

For my meditation teacher, who is an ever-present guide, always encouraging me from within to expand into greater and greater realms of presence in the everyday moments of life.

Table of Contents

PART THREE

LIVING IN AUTHENTICITY

List of poetry by S'Marie Young in order of appearance:

Foreword

*M*ore often than not, the wise person is able to learn from the mistakes of others. Life intended every individual to succeed. We are destined for success. But what does success mean to you? You will achieve success in your terms, which may mean, you could be a successful failure. In either case you become what you focus on and believe as true. That's the way of life. Emergence presents personal examples that are transparent for immediate transfer to actual and practical use and offers a path of fulfillment and confidence that is easy to follow and simple to do.

In this thought-provoking book, S'Marie Young lays out a plan by which any serious-minded individual can follow to its completion. Starting from her early years to present day, the detailed lessons unfold in chronological clarity, in an open and introspective way that causes us to look deep within ourselves. Through stories that speak volumes, we are prompted to move in a new direction—one that could be serendipitous. Our inner creative child always remains within us and we can tap that creativity whenever we call upon it. Using personal, candid, real-life examples as a catalyst for change, disillusionment and hurt turn into learning experiences.

From years as an introvert, reserved and unassuming which blocked from her own communication channel to the surrounding world, the author steps boldly forward with her actions and guides us to move more swiftly to gratified accomplishment. Not an easy path for most, unless following the guidelines of someone who has walked in those shoes.

Whether the past is uncomfortable or pleasant, there are jewels to be gleaned. Dwelling on the past can rob us of the here and now—the precious present. Knowing this is called Emotional Intelligence. Mistakes are only steps which allow us to reach a destination more swiftly and consistently. Using her past experiences as lessons from which to grow, we gain vicarious insights so as to learn, but without the pain and anguish of personal experience.

Word power is also discussed. The power of words can make or break a deal or relationship. A realization that words actually form the fabric of our future is tactfully addressed. The choices we make in choosing our words have a significant impact. When we change the things we say about the things we do, the experience changes. When we change the things we say about those with whom we associate, the relationship changes. After reading Emergence, you may find yourself choosing words differently.

Substitute praise for condemnation. This sounds simple, but habits sometimes get in the way. Behavior, attitudes and even ethics and values enter in to it. The point being that, if a new and different experience is desired, one that is more productive and more rewarding, what we think and what we say about it is a good place to start.

Honesty, responsibility and trust are all elements of building a solid foundation for a successful personal and professional life. How we address these issues are directly revealed in the outer world reflecting the experiences and relationships as a mirror reflects an image.

In Emergence, we find ourselves engaged in the author's principles and guidelines to fulfillment. Depending upon how they are used, they can be flexible or as unyielding as our resistance can be. The way we see ourselves is the way we greet the world, and that is exactly the way the world greets us back. Follow this path and watch the new you emerge. You will enjoy this continually unfolding process moment by moment.

JAMES MELTON, PhD, Speaker and Author

PART ONE

FINDING *Your* VOICE: STANDING *in Your* TRUTH

Chapter One

WHO WE ARE
and
WHAT WE SAY

Roots: Where We've Come From

The Child's Soul Journey

I hope you will go out and let stories, that is life, happen to you, and that you will work with these stories from your life—not someone else's life—water them with your blood and tears and your laughter till they bloom, till you yourself burst into bloom. That is the work. The only work. ~ CLARISSA PINKOLA ESTÉS

Let us begin at the beginning, with my own inner child, Sally. Blue was my favorite color; it matched my eyes. My favorite outfit at six was a white leather skirt, and a sky blue sweater, with a furry hand warmer, that felt like a silky rabbit. Not sure why I needed a hand warmer in sunny San Diego, but I loved it. I wore that outfit until the waist of the skirt was so tight I couldn't breathe. I wore it to parties and to church, which we attended every Sunday.

After Sunday school and the service was over, we would join my grandparents and go to the diner across the street to have hamburgers and chocolate milkshakes, or fried chicken as a special treat. That was the best part of the day!

I grew up in a traditional family of four. My dad was from the Midwest, and my mom from Montana. They both ended up in San Diego after college, and were fixed up by church members who thought they were both too old to be single. My mom was five years older than my dad. The family joke was that she refused to pick him up hitchhiking as she passed him in her nice Chevy sedan. Although it's common now, a thirty-five-year-old bride was old in the mid nineteen fifties. They wasted no time, and I was born a year and a quarter later.

One Sunday, after the diner, we stopped at a bookstore. As we looked around, a shining blue bracelet caught my eye. It was shimmering and calling to me. The clerk took it out of the case and clasped it around my wrist. I was instantly attached, and my parents agreed to buy it for me. I wore it out of the store, mesmerized by its beauty. Settled at home, my mom took a closer look at it. She moaned, and said "Oh no, in the blue inlets are images of Mother Mary—you can't keep that." I was crushed, but no amount of screaming and crying shifted the outcome. It was the divine feminine, and she had to go. My parents suggested I give it to my friend down the street who attended mass. Tearfully, I let her go, and it took forty years for her to return to my life.

Inside each of us is a glorious, innocent, wise, and supremely free nugget that is our true self. Somehow, along the way, this nugget of truth gets hidden underneath layers of who we think we are and who others want us to be. This essence of us becomes unrecognizable, even to ourselves. It doesn't disappear, but it is elusive. At some point in our lives, the longing to know our true self can become unbearable, and it is at this crossroads that we turn within, and the journey begins. Arrival at this crossroads often happens when outer circumstances cause us to become disillusioned, or hurt us enough to force a change. Sometimes life and relationships seems shallow, and we feel empty. There is no meaning to it all. In this day and age, most people are working too hard, running too fast, and every waking second is monopolized by technology. There isn't a quiet moment to just be. In between though, there are nanoseconds of silence, and the inner voice shouts out—I'm here! Listen! I'm waiting.

I am sharing my journey with you, in the hopes that it inspires you to begin your own journey, or to celebrate your progress if you are well on your way. I've mixed short stories of my own experiences and poetry that I wrote as I found my history and my voice. Interspersed is wisdom that I've gained through the process and systems and people who helped along the way. Self-transformation, once begun, is a journey that never ends. The scenery just gets more beautiful, and the ability to appreciate, and even enjoy it grows. It is a labor of love.

Whether we know it consciously or not, that little girl or boy we once were is still with us, and has a much greater influence over our lives than most of us realize. The child's soul journey is to find and reclaim missing parts of us that were lost along the way. Cultivating a relationship with our inner child by listening and dialoguing with that long buried part of us is a way to reclaim our power. Giving him or her a chance to speak is part of the process of unleashing our own adult voice. Going back and retrieving memories of early experiences gives us clues as to why we have difficulty now speaking up in a direct and powerful way. It can also show us where we left the trail and wandered away from our soul's deepest purpose, revealing long buried dreams.

As children, free expression of our feelings and thoughts was often discouraged and sometimes downright forbidden. Unfortunately, "Children should be seen and not heard," is a rule that persists. It's not always so overt, but rather in the everyday busyness, adults forget to listen and respect the spontaneous and clear communication of a child. In response, as children, we either got louder and more insistent that we be heard, or we withdrew into our shells, feeling that what we had to say wasn't worthy. Whatever coping mechanism we used, we repeated it until it became habitual. Once a pattern was established, we lost the power of choice. As each year passes, more rules of socialization are imbibed and less and less of the spontaneous freedom of the child shines through. When we ourselves become the adult, there are so many layers of enculturation and survival skills, we no longer remember the soul of the child, and we lose our precious connection.

Why Look Back?

*I*f we want to be the main influencer of the direction our lives take, then we must learn to speak so that others will listen and take us seriously. First, we have to take ourselves seriously! This means making a commitment to do the work necessary to affect a change within. For only when we change what's inside, will we see a change in the outside world. Part of this process involves gaining clarity about where we come from—our earliest childhood experiences. We are not to wallow in the repressed pain that sometimes surfaces, but to acknowledge it, comfort our little child, and let it go. We retrieve our inner child from the depths and begin our soul journey.

Parts of the journey are uncomfortable, and downright painful, so you may ask—why dredge up the past? Why not just let it be? Inner work can seem a waste of time, and run contrary to staying in the present moment. Dwelling in the past can rob us of the present, but unresolved childhood issues control the present. Proactively contemplating memories for clues to present behaviors that may stem from unresolved past hurts is different than playing old reels over and over, and sinking into an emotional morass. To do this, consider the following questions:

Action Step:

- Have you accomplished everything you set out to do?

- Are you living the life of your dreams?

- Do you have an incessant inner critic that keeps you from really going for it, or beats you down every time you step out too far?

If you are not satisfied with your answer to any of those questions, your inner child may be screaming out to get your attention. Listen.

Until we come to accept the past, no matter how painful, it will haunt us, affecting everything we do and how we perceive the world. The soul's journey is to uncover the gems that are hidden right inside. It is the work of bringing together all our scattered bones and parts, and weaving them into a cohesive whole that reveals the masterpiece that is "I." Then, we discover and serve our true soul's purpose with every action we take. There is freedom in acceptance. Over time gratitude for our past emerges, and we are at peace. Our lives become aligned with who we really are, and we make a real difference in the world around us.

If we don't do this work, whatever we avoid ends up having more power over us than anything else. When I first began to look inside myself in my early thirties, the therapist that facilitated the process had a poster on her wall with a quote by Marcel Proust that helped me through my journey: "The real voyage of discovery consists not in seeking new landscapes, but in having new eyes." As you embark on this voyage of self-discovery, my wish for you, is to be blessed with new eyes.

Family dynamics and early interactions put into place habitual patterns of speaking, feeling, and acting that can last a lifetime, unless we become aware of them and have a strong desire to change. Even then, it can be difficult to interrupt patterns that are ingrained from a young age. We often have the mistaken belief that this is who we are, and it is impossible to change. No, it's not easy, but it is definitely possible to transform ourselves into high functioning human beings. It's important to gain the ability to observe and change our inner state. This is emotional intelligence.

Making Peace with Our Past

How could we forget those ancient myths. . . the myths about dragons that at the last moment are transformed into princesses? Perhaps all the dragons in our lives are princesses who are only wanting to see us act, just once with beauty and courage. Perhaps everything that frightens us, in its deepest essence, something helpless that wants our love. ~Rainer Maria Rilke

From my earliest memories, I had a difficult time standing in my own truth. I was a shy child, and I had a younger sister who was outgoing and talkative. While I was too reserved to ask for what I needed most of the time, she demanded—and got attention. I was two years older and always mature for my age; she was the baby of our extended family and treated as such. Even though I tried to act grown-up, this must have caused some jealousy and resentment on my part. A favorite family story is that I tipped over my sister's crib—with her in it!

My most significant memories of communication between my parents and me, involved me being deathly afraid of asking for things that I wanted or needed, but thought they might have a problem with. I was never able to ask directly. As I got older, and my body was changing, this pattern became more entrenched. My mom taught me about the birds and the bees by bringing home a book from the church library, which she read with me. I asked no questions afterward. I learned about menstruation in a movie shown to sixth grade girls.

I thought all the other girls in my grade six class were shaving their legs, except me. One Sunday morning, I refused to go to church. When mom asked why, I said I couldn't wear a dress because my legs were too hairy. She just laughed, and said if I wanted the ongoing hassle of shaving—go right ahead. I was thrilled! I hadn't asked directly, but I took a stand and expressed my embarrassment about my hairy legs. It worked! Mom didn't judge me or yell, or refuse a genuine desire. I wish I could say that this experience changed me, and made it easier to express sensitive issues, but it did not. This fear of speaking out has haunted me throughout my life.

Being shy, I needed people to ask questions to draw me out. My parents were very loving, but reserved. My mom was a teacher, so after making dinner, she would often grade papers until it was time for bed. Dad was a probation officer, and I remember him arriving home with a bag of Fritos to go with his beer or scotch and water. He would settle down to relax behind the newspaper, which I'd swat away when I was little. Looking back, from a fairly young age, I carried on a private life filled with untellable stories of events and feelings they knew nothing about. With both parents working, I was at home alone many afternoons, and I loved the freedom that gave me. I'll share some of those untellable stories as we go. Of course, in retrospect, I wonder what all the secrecy was about. We'll explore that too in the pages following.

What do we do when rummaging through our past brings up anger, resentment, guilt, shame, grief, or sorrow? We allow it free expression, without judgment. Now, I don't mean a free-for-all with anyone within hearing distance! You might lose a few relationships that way. Share with a trusted friend or therapist, but mainly with yourself through journaling, movement, energy work, or even screaming in the car.

I've journaled my dreams since I was a young adult, and one of the most healing expressions for me is writing poetry, which I've shared throughout these pages. Poetry is a language of metaphor, similar to the symbolic messages we receive in dreams. Both reach us on a level deeper than ordinary consciousness. Dreams and metaphor come from and speak to the creative side of the brain, bypassing the logical mind that rationalizes everything. We may not understand our dreams or even our poetry, but they are sorting out and working through the experiences of our lives. The more we encourage and listen to our dreams and creative expressions, the more they will reveal to us.

When repressed feelings and thoughts are written, it brings them to the light, and diffuses their power. It is in the dark recesses that they do the most damage. When we see them written, we witness them from a distance. Space and time intervene and we get a clearer perspective. Paradoxically, when we write down our deepest heart's desires, they become intentions and goals, and are imbued with power. But, as long as those subconscious beliefs about ourselves are hidden, they sabotage us and win the day. Our self-image is created from early imprints of how we were treated and what we were told about our self. We think it's who we really are, when actually it is just reflection that we absorbed and took to be real. Sadly, we become attached to this false image. The personality forms to maintain and defend and protect that image we hold of ourselves.

It's not only our distant past that we need to come to terms with, but the stubbed toes, arrows, and stone throwing we have endured along the way. There are bound to be stuck arrows and shards remaining, surrounded by a hard pack of mud. They slow us down or speed us up, and give us a hitch in our gait. Every new relationship seems to be a replay of the past, no matter how many times we swear we won't get messed up with another one like that! It is said that we marry one of, or a combination of our parents, and our relationships are just mirrors of our past. Until we wake up and deal with the original wounding, we keep scraping the same old spots, singing the same old blues, and adding more layers concealing our essence. Or, we clam up into a protective shell and give up on intimate relationships. As a close friend of mine says, "my picker is broken!" There comes a point in life, where for many of us, it's easier to remain unattached, than to risk yet another heartbreak.

Making peace with the past means accepting what brought us to this point, and loving who we've become in spite of, and because of those experiences. It means letting the past remain there, and entering each present moment anew, with fresh perspective. There is a lightness of being, a joyfulness that bubbles forth. A trust in the goodness of life becomes established.

There can be profound sadness and grief when we let go of the stories we've told ourselves about the past, coming face to face with broken innocence. Children have a coping mechanism of assuming responsibility for everything that happens. Seeing clearly that it wasn't our fault can be a sharp awakening.

Gatekeeper, the poem that follows expresses raw thoughts and feelings surrounding my broken innocence and sharp awakening into reality of existence.

Gatekeeper

The little girl, long forgotten, cried out in pain.
What about me—don't I deserve forgiveness, too?
The broken pieces came together,
a strong woman, save one gashing wound.
Shards of worthlessness still remain.

Sharp reminders there's still a job to do.
Help her find her voice and speak the truth.

I am pure and innocent,
A budding flower ready to bloom.
I am the lone rose, velvet and soft,
Plucked before its time.

I am the full bloom rose,
Wilted and spent,
Petals floating in the air.
I am the cool ocean breeze,
And the harsh desert air.
I am the fluttering of blinds
And the stillness of night.
I am the stuff of your dreams,
The pictures in your albums.
I dole out memories as you will have them.

I am the gatekeeper; I protect you with my life.
I am your tears you cry for no reason.
I am your bladder when it locks tight.

I took responsibility when it was not mine to hold.
I drug you through the mud,
Trying to cleanse my soul.

I am your enthusiasm, your drive.
In your independent nature,
I take pride.
I allow you no slack, the journey must continue.
To exonerate me
Is your responsibility.

I speak to you from ancient memory.
We've been here before.
Leaving an unfinished dream.

We will endure, you and I,
Goldiggers we are in our search for the truth.
I'll reveal it to you someday soon.
Long after it matters.

Expression and Repression:
Gems from My Past

My journey through expressing myself has been a dichotomy. On the one hand, I'm an introvert, and quiet. On the other hand, there was always something in me that liked to perform. The fear of speaking out seemed to disappear when I was on stage, so to speak. There's a home movie of me at about three years old, silent back then, putting on a show in the alcove where the television was normally housed. I was staging my own theatrics. Seeing this film confounds the picture I carry of myself as a child too shy to talk to strangers. I like the term ambivert, having characteristics of both introvert and extrovert.

My parents took my sister and me to plays in an outdoor theatre in Balboa Park, the Starlight Opera. It was mesmerizing watching the actors and listening to the orchestra under the night stars. Directly in the flight path, the actors would freeze and the music would pause when the jets flew low overhead, landing at nearby Lindbergh Field. We saw classics like *Peter Pan*, *The King and I*, *Camelot* and *Annie Get Your Gun*. I can still see Tinkerbell in her shimmering tutu flying across the stage. I also vividly remember seeing the magical snow maiden ballerinas decked out in white in *The Nutcracker Suite* ballet at the Civic Theatre, in downtown San Diego one year at Christmastime.

Books opened up a vast world for me. My mother was a primary school teacher, and she read to me from the time I was a baby. She said I taught myself to read, I think it was *Green Eggs and Ham* by Dr. Seuss. I would grab the book and start reading aloud, even though the book was upside down. Eventually, I associated the letters with words, and it was no longer just memorization of the story. My favorite time in school was when the teacher would read a chapter a day from a novel. Her voice and expressiveness brought the characters alive. Even more exciting was when we got to order paperback books. I was very taken by the descriptions and couldn't wait to read the stories. I always read beyond my grade level, and eventually took books from my parents' shelves. Books taught me things far beyond my years; yet, there was a part of me that understood, even though I had not had the real life experience. I am still enchanted with the places a book can take me.

Another childhood memory dents my shy image. I was in fourth grade, and we were on the cafeteria stage, assigned to make up skits in group of three. I had so much fun creating and performing. I remember being surprised at myself that there was no fear. Contrast this to the sixth grade humiliation of trying out for glee club and being the only girl in the entire school who did not pass the audition. They said it was because my voice was too deep, but I think it was more about inheriting my dad's monotone. The embarrassment was quickly relieved when I got to practice gymnastics instead on the parallel bars with my favorite teacher, Mr. Blair. The lasting scar was that I would not sing aloud until I was in my late thirties and began to chant at a meditation center.

Even though my father was a probation officer, he was very tolerant of my rebellious nature and strong opinions. We would often get in heated debates, and he never yelled, criticized, or told me to shut up. I felt respected and that my thoughts and opinions were of value. He helped me build confidence and learn how to interact with men. One of the main ways we connected after I moved out of the house, until he died, was through the discussion of finances. Being in sales, a commission only business, for most of my life, there were often long gaps between paychecks and he always was there to smooth things out. It wasn't until I was in my thirties that I could fully appreciate and respect his conservative and smart financial savvy and commitment to saving and planning for the future. I could then understand that this was his way of showing his love for me, and I felt it strongly. He said, "I love you" once in awhile, but his actions spoke much louder than his words.

What We Say Is Important, and How We Say It Is Even More Important

Sibling Rivalry

I have to say, this is the most challenging, and perhaps the most significant relationship of my life. Relationship partners mirrored her, rather than a parent. My sister, Kate and I have struggled with each other all our lives. At times we have been close friends, at other, estranged sisters. Always, I love her. Sometimes, I can't stand to be around her. When we were kids, we fought—teeth, nails, fists and feet. When we got too old for that, words and distance became weapons of choice.

We are two years apart, the only siblings in our family. Power struggles started early. Our well-meaning parents created competition between us by making sure everything was always equal—one never got anything without the other getting the same or equal value. Real life doesn't work like that.

My sister and I are complete opposites. She's extroverted; I'm more of an introvert. She shares freely her feelings and her life stories. Most things have to be drawn out of me. We are on opposite sides politically. I often felt overwhelmed by her big energy field. I imagine she has felt abandoned or ignored by me.

At the core of all of our conflicts was the fear and anger of being controlled. I saw her as always trying to control my time by making demands about time—when I should be somewhere, and admonishing me to be on time. She got infuriated at me for telling her what to do, seeing me as stuck in my role of big sister and never treating her as an equal or good enough as she is.

I reacted passive-aggressively many times after agreeing to be somewhere at a time she specified, when I thought it was unreasonable. Instead of saying no, I would fume about it, and resent her. Inevitably, my stress would create a situation that prevented me from or gave me an excuse not to be on time. That was my way of getting even.

When she would get mad at me, her reactions felt like blaming. When I made a comment about her, told her what to do, or offended her in some way, she would call me on it then and there, and I'd usually react defensively or sarcastically. But that was not the end of it. I received so many letters and emails over the years, outlining the latest way I wronged her, as well as a litany of incidents going back years. They felt like spankings!

I often said that no matter if we lived in the same house, town, or a few hours away, I could feel her angry energy coming at me after a fight. I was afraid of it, and would spend hours or days in crafting a response to each accusation that wouldn't incite her further. Just like with my sister, in past relationships with men, their anger knocked me off my truth so fast, I couldn't discern what was real. I spent a lot of time defending myself and wondering if I was really as bad as I was being portrayed. Eventually, I worked through my fear of others anger, and my responses became immediate and scathing.

Bottom line: she had something that I wanted, assertiveness (often more like aggressiveness); and I projected on her the anger I disowned. Being afraid to bring my parents bad news, I had her do it, including when I was thirty years old and left my husband for another man!

Her words were quick, brash, and often explosive. Definitely attention getting. My words were slower to form, quiet, and hesitant, except when angry. I was not the one speaking out in class, until high school, and even then, I was shy.

Owning the Power of Words

As a young adult, just out of high school, I attended a small, local finishing school to learn tearoom modeling. For graduation, we modeled at the Denny's a few blocks away, twirling and explaining our outfits to families over milkshakes, burgers, and fries. The same thing happened there, as in childhood (even though the setting was embarrassing); I loved talking to all those people! From there, I was able to get a job in a hotel boutique doing tearoom modeling in the restaurant. Far from a tearoom, it was a steamy steakhouse and bar that was a popular lunchtime hangout for contractors and businessmen. Again, I got an education far beyond my years, learning to banter with tables of men enjoying cocktails with their meal—selling outfits and jewelry for their girlfriends or wives, or both. It got me through a few years of college and my first year in real estate.

From outfits and trinkets, I used my experience with that rough and tumble crowd to go into the land business, where ninety-eight percent of my clients were men. Ray Forrest, a contractor I met at the restaurant, was building his own office building next door, and eventually I went to work for him. I learned to lease office space and sell apartment buildings. Ray mentored me through my first land transaction, a site for twenty-eight condominiums. I was hooked on the intricacies and excitement of negotiating land deals.

One way I overcame my shyness was to join a Toastmasters club in my twenties to conquer my fear of public speaking. Toastmasters International teaches members leadership skills and public speaking through crafting and delivering speeches and active participation in meeting roles and activities. At that time, I only gave the first four out of a ten speech manual, but it was enough to help my confidence in speaking in front of groups. From early on, part of the services I provided was to speak in front of planning board and city council public hearings to advocate project approval on behalf of the landowner or developer. At first I was terrified, and I remember stumbling on words, my voice low and shaking, my face bright red. I think it helped to get project approvals because they felt so sorry for me! Toastmasters also helped tremendously when I started a new career in coaching and training. Starting over, I gave the first ten speeches and earned the designation "competent communicator." The change in confidence and delivery between the first and tenth speech was vast.

A large part of my real estate business was conducted over the phone. Most of my clients were not local. To find both buyers and sellers, the best method I found was to call and talk to them directly. This meant I had to be genuine and quick on my feet, because most people, including me, are wary of people selling things over the phone. I was selling myself as a professional and had to establish rapport quickly, or I would get shut down or the person merely hung up. Relationships were developed because they wanted my expertise, and I wanted to serve them by finding the right property or buyer. There were many instances that I worked with people and completed transactions without ever meeting in person. Phone and written communication was our only way to communicate.

Sales negotiations are a particular kind of communication skill. The real estate transaction has inherent conflict. The buyer wants to buy as cheaply as possible, and the seller wants to sell as high as possible. Ultimately, both have the same goal, of transferring ownership from one to the other, so the negotiation is to find a meeting place, where both parties are satisfied. It is the role of the broker to facilitate agreement of that meeting place. Once found, that is only the beginning. There are many hurdles to cross, like financing and the development approval process, which sometimes takes over a year, plus factoring in changing market conditions in a lengthy transaction.

Maintaining direct, clear communication between the parties as a go-between was a critical part of my job. I sometimes felt like I was trying to mediate between two bulls fighting. Most of the time, problems could be worked out, but sometimes the impasse was so large, there was no solution, except to cancel. With so much time and effort involved, that is hard on everyone. I always dreaded delivering bad news, but inevitably, if I had a problem communicating something, it would create problems in the whole deal, so I had to learn to choose my words carefully and deliver them in a way that did not create conflict. Being calm, factual and direct, with compassion doesn't change the news, but it makes it easier to accept. Listening carefully is the most important part of any negotiation.

My shyness came out in being afraid to express my deepest feelings and truths. A group that helped me get comfortable sharing my feelings, was Al-Anon, a twelve-step support group for those who are affected by another's disease of alcoholism. Being in an atmosphere of nonjudgment, no interruption, and no feedback helped me to discern my own feelings from someone else's and to articulate them effectively. It also helped me to be responsible for my own words and actions in relationships, and to let go of assuming responsibility for others.

In my current profession as a coach, I have gained even more appreciation for verbal communication. Now, rather than acting as a communication bridge between two people, I facilitate a bridge to the inner self. The skills are similar, that of curiosity, intuition, and asking powerful questions, only now they are directed inward to help people access their own wisdom. Whether it is to coach someone to peak success in his or her business, or help people stand in their truth, it all begins with inner awareness. There is nothing more empowering than speaking the truth of your heart.

I've often been grateful for the erase and re-record feature on many voicemail systems, when I leave a message that becomes long and repetitive or confused because I didn't think about what I was going to say before dialing the phone. Wouldn't it be nice if we had the ability to erase an outburst we later regret, or when we wish we could eat our words because their reception is opposite of what we intended? Words make up our thoughts and speech, and therefore, create the world we live in. The great spiritual texts impart this wisdom. In the *Chandogya Upanishad*, it is said:

> If there were no speech, neither right nor wrong would be known; neither true nor false; neither good nor bad; neither pleasant nor unpleasant. Speech makes us understand all this. Meditate on speech. (VII, ii. I)

With this immense power of speech, it is of paramount importance that we think before we speak, and choose our words carefully. When we discipline our thoughts, and pause before speaking, we gain control over what comes out of our mouth. It has been said that the tongue is our best friend or our worst enemy. We get to choose which it will be.

One of the best ways to make our tongue our best friend is to connect to the great-heart before we speak. Simply taking a breath and directing it to our heart, then letting our words form from there can make a big difference in our choice of words and the tone in which they are delivered.

Becoming aware of how we talk to ourselves gives us the ability to change the negative beliefs and self-talk that sabotage our dreams and goals. It doesn't matter what the words are, if the corresponding thought or emotion is incongruent, they are what will win. Making sure our words match our tone, and are aligned with our deepest heart's desire, is a great way to connect with the world and others in an authentic manner. When we do this, the world responds to us in the same way.

It takes discernment and discipline to know if we are speaking in a way that will just perpetuate anger and negativity, or if expressing it is a right and powerful way to transform ourselves, others, and circumstances that need to be changed. Speaking out is a necessary part of finding our voice. Pausing and connecting to our breath allows a moment to get clear about what we want to say, and our motivation for speaking up. Do we want control over someone else? Are we being fair or judgmental? We can witness our state and determine if we have self-control, or if an emotional reaction has overtaken us. There are reactive behaviors like blaming or groveling that cast us in the role of perpetrator or victim. Whichever role we are playing, we have lost our power to choose our destiny. Our inner state affects the way we communicate. Whether we feel agitated, calm, cowardly or courageous—we convey that to others energetically. Our state affects others. How many times have you been feeling down, and been completely transformed by a smile or an excited, happy friend sharing good news? And the opposite, have you been relaxed and then felt tense and uncomfortable after just being in ear shot of an angry exchange? Other people's emotions can have lasting effects on us.

There are habitual patterns of communication that we bring to every interaction. Most of the time, we remain unaware of these automatic responses that were set up early on in our lives. We often have no idea that as we communicate, we are reacting to others with responses that come from deep beneath the surface. Connecting to our own heart and really listening to what is going on inside is the foundation of authentic, powerful communication. If we have that kind of self-awareness, we can begin to speak from the truth of our own heart. We will then know that what we are saying is congruent with what we are feeling, so the inherent power of our words is much greater. We will have more control over our responses to circumstances; and, therefore, we have the power to shift our circumstances to fulfill our deepest heart's desires. It all begins within.

The Four Gateways of Speech

When we stand in our truth and speak from that grounded place, we reclaim the exuberance and vitality of a child. We take personal responsibility for what is ours and let others keep what's theirs. We speak with respect for our self and the other person. When we are no longer caught up in the web of our past, or fear about the future, we speak from the present moment, and our words ring true and appropriate.

There are four gateways of speech that come from the Sufi or Buddhist tradition and have been adopted with minor variations by many paths of yoga and conscious living. Checking in with these gateways before speaking is a good way to develop communication that is well spoken and well received. Here are the four gateways of speech to pass through before opening our mouth:

1. Are these words true?

2. Are they necessary?

3. Are they timely?

4. Are they kind?

Now that is quite a test. If we all opened and passed through every one of those gates before talking, there would sure be a lot less idle conversation, gossip, misunderstanding, and conflict.

Often, we have the toughest time communicating with those are closest to us. When there is a long history, especially with family, it is difficult to break patterns of communication or miscommunication. Expectations are projected onto every conversation, based on the past. Family dynamics also come into play—yelling may have been prominent, or a rigidity of maintaining politeness, or concealment of feelings. Our parents might have encouraged or discouraged curiosity and debate. It seems nothing can bring me face to face with old misbehavior patterns more than time with family!

Action Step:

- What were your family dynamics?

- Who was/is your most challenging family member?

- In thinking about your most intimate relation ship, which familiar relationship or relation ships does it remind you of?

- If you could say anything you want to this person or persons, what would you want to express?

- Write a letter, or allow it's free expression in another medium. Keep it, burn it, or share it; whatever is appropriate for you.

- What is holding you back from the conversation?

- Ask yourself, What would happen if I shifted my perception of this person?

Honesty in Relationships:
Is it Fact or Fantasy?

*R*omantic relationships are one of the most difficult areas of our lives to remain objective. We are blinded by dreams, hopes, expectations, and chemistry. The fear of being alone causes us to put on glasses that are gradient: they invent and magnify wonderful qualities we are looking for, and they diminish and hide qualities that are suspect. We also create an image of who we think the other wants us to be, and try our best to become that person. It takes honest self-inquiry, and frank discussions to get our heads out of the clouds and grounded in reality. The problem is, we want him or her to be the one so much that we avoid looking at and talking about important issues that are vital to a successful relationship. We instead choose to ignore the warning signs, and sometimes it is years and children later when we realize we aren't with who we thought we were, and neither is our partner.

We can see this personified in the online love-scammers. These are usually foreigners wanting to con women (maybe men too), by striking up conversations through social media or dating sites. They can be very smooth, look good, and say all the right things, offering compliments and love and talk of a beautiful future together. They often play the sympathy card by being widowed and raising children alone. They prey on people who are lonely, and so won't notice the spelling errors, and clues that their profile doesn't exist in the real system. I hate to think of the hundreds, if not thousands of broken hearts and emptied wallets there are out there. People who have been swindled by their own unwillingness to see the truth, reality as it is, not as they would like it to be.

I got married the first time, after finding out that my husband-to-be carried on with a previous girlfriend for three years, while in a relationship with me, after telling me when we met that they had split up and were no longer seeing each other. I was young and was determined to have what I wanted, which was him, not realizing that there were deep fissures beneath our vows. We bicycled, golfed, attended football games together, but there was not much intimacy in our conversations. We did not know how to share our true selves with one another, or even with our self.

We enjoyed drinking with friends at our favorite bar. At first, it was me who started early on Friday afternoons. By the time he walked in, I was well on my way, and he would get mad, telling me it brought up painful childhood memories of his mother hanging off a bar stool (she stopped drinking before I met her, and we stayed in contact until she died). At one point, roles changed—when the drunk-driving law lowered the legal limit to .08 in California. That straightened me up fast. I became the designated driver when we were out.

More often, it was now me waiting at home, getting angrier by the minute. When he walked in, I'd berate him and tell him not to expect me to bail him out of jail for driving drunk. We both had the disease of alcoholism in our family history, and we were manifesting it now firsthand. Each family member has a role, and the sober one often acts crazier than the drinker, trying to control the uncontrollable by making threats or acting out in revenge. I never heard of Al-Anon then, the support group for friends and families of alcoholics. We grew farther and farther apart, until I couldn't even stand for him to touch me.

Too afraid to confront my unhappiness or the prospect of being alone, I welcomed the advances of one of his drinking buddies. After three months of sneaking around, my husband picked up the extension late one night, as I was listening to an office voicemail from my lover proclaiming his love. From peak rage that had my heart beating full speed, to tears asking me to stay, he left for work the next morning. I packed my trunk and drove away, never to return.

I knew immediately on some level, that I'd made a huge mistake in the way I departed. It took me three years to get out of the even worse relationship I'd jumped into; it took many years to let go of the shame. Eventually, my ex-husband called, during a short time of sobriety in Alcoholics Anonymous, to apologize and take responsibility for his part of the mess. I let him know that life had punished me severely for the error of my ways. We had lunch once and spoke sporadically, until I last saw him, a few days before he died. An old mutual friend told me after the memorial service that he died from cirrhosis of the liver and hepatitis, accelerated by drinking.

I vowed to myself never again to be so afraid of sharing who I am, and what I'm honestly feeling, and above all to leave honorably if a relationship needs to end.

The following poems illustrate some points on my journey to standing in my truth, vacillating between placating victim and passive-aggressive shrew!

A Bleeding Heart

I've got to breathe, get my own fresh air.
The room is so stale with you blowing smoke.
I've just got to leave.

There's no room for me here.
Your energy fills the space,
And scares me, it's so big and strong.

Your story is firm and true.
Mine disappears under the weight
Of the firmly held conviction, so convincingly told.

It must be true, he wouldn't lie.
He might leave over this, so he says.
I must change or risk being alone.
How do I change?
I don't understand what he says.
It might be true, I don't know.

But I don't see it, and he makes me mad.
Let's kiss and make up, and bury the pain.
He doesn't mean it, he was just mad.

He loves me so much, I know this is true.
I love him too.
But the air is so stale, I can no longer breathe.
I don't feel anymore, I have to leave.

My heart is deeply hurt.
I don't even know the depth of the pain.
Wounded by his anger, buried by my rage.
Underneath lies a bleeding heart,
Crying out for love.

Flowers and Nice

I fall asleep to my anger and rage,
But it comes out
In covert ways.
I'm so nice, but underneath,
The bitch is brewing some bitter tea.
Sweetened just enough you can't taste the poison
Until it's too late.

I cover it up with flowers and nice,
But underneath there's a cauldron of lice.
You can't see them, but they itch you in little ways.
They're so small you don't even know you're being attacked.

One day you come home and your bags are packed.
Get the hell out, and don't come back!

I hit you broadside,
And you don't even know what you did to deserve such a blow.

I loved you so much, all flowers and nice.
But underneath, I was planning your demise.
You hit me head on, and I just smiled.
My secret life, you'll never know.

I beguile other men, and bask in the glow.
All the while, giving flowers and nice.
The bitch is here, so watch your backside.
My name is Sally, and I'm a fucking bitch!

Forgiveness and
Self-Responsibility

One of the most empowering ways of using our voice is for a genuine apology. It is hard for most of us, but developing this skill has many rewards. Taking responsibility for our actions is difficult, especially when they've created negative consequences for our self or someone else. Whether it's low self-esteem, fear of looking bad, or of retribution, the resulting cover-up or shifting of blame carries far greater repercussions than the disowned action. Because we can't let it go. It leaves discomfort in the relationship with the one we've hurt, and it sits within our mind as guilt or shame, often popping up years later as a painful memory, or replayed in a new relationship with similar dynamics.

Blaming is self-protection. We may feel better at first, but the guilt it causes is a high price to pay. It also undermines our power over our own lives, putting us in the role of victim.

How do we become free from this cycle? A famous quote from a popular movie in the seventies is "Love means never having to say you're sorry." This statement may sound good, but it really isn't true. A measure of true love for ourselves and others is the ability to say "I'm sorry," and own up to our words and actions, and their consequences.

In late 2014, the national news reported on the investigation into torture and abuse that the CIA inflicted on prisoners in the years after 9/11. It was interesting to watch the reactions of the politicians. Who was taking responsibility and owning up, and who was trying to sweep it under the carpet? Who deflected and justified by talking about how evil the victims were, and that it was "the only way" to get it done? In the public discourse, who blamed government and "them," and who shared responsibility as citizens who have a vote, a consciousness and a voice?

I look at this drama as a lesson and a mirror for our own life. When we do something wrong, or make a mistake, how do we react—hiding it, defensively making excuses, blaming the accuser or someone else—or do we own up and admit to our wrongdoings?

In my childhood, and well into adult life, it was mortifying to be caught for mistakes. I was ashamed and afraid of apologizing. One day as a third-grader, I walked by my teacher's desk, knocking a vase over as I brushed against it. I kept on walking and didn't look back, not saying a word! When she asked for hand up for who soaked all her papers—mine stayed glued to my lap. She could probably see who did it, by my bright red face, and she didn't choose to belabor it, thankfully for me. It happened again as a twenty-two-year-old very green real estate agent. A colleague and I were using the manager's office for a project; I spilled a glass of water. This time I did clean it up, but I did not tell him what I did. When my colleague told him, he angrily confronted me about his ruined files. I was mortified. Beet red and ashamed of myself, I apologized. His anger wasn't so much flared by what I did, but more so for not taking responsibility for the blunder. That incident helped me to change, but until I realized it's not shameful to make mistakes, and it's a wonderful opportunity to learn and grow, it didn't get much easier to own up.

We, as a country and as individuals, like to look good at all times. We have an image to uphold, that of being the saviors and good guys on this earth. It is difficult to admit that we have more in common with our enemies than we would like to believe. Silence is complicit and we have been complicit too many times. It is easy to look in retrospect and say we should have done something, but even today there is complicity at many of the atrocities going on in the world. Where in your own life are you being complicit? Where is it difficult for you to own up and say I'm sorry? I have found that taking responsibility by admitting my wrongdoings and apologizing has been humbling and freeing, once I get over the embarrassment. It allows me to forgive myself and move on, without the extra weight of guilt. I gain more energy to devote to my priorities, and usually, my relationship with the recipient improves.

What about the times you truly have been wronged, especially as the victim of abuse or crime? Children often take responsibility for bad things that happen. As I began to review my childhood from the eyes of an adult, I could see that I took far too much responsibility. There were many instances where the adults in my life were asleep. Although I was not a victim of a crime, or abuse, things happened that I was too young for, and I took full responsibility as a preteen. I thought I was all grown up and that I had a choice, not realizing the influence that older teens and young adults had on me. Sometimes taking full responsibility means being strong enough to admit to being taken advantage of, and not having control over everything. It means admitting that someone else was at fault, because they had power over us. In these cases, it's about forgiving ourselves.

When you know you were the clear victim, there is justified anger, rage, and thoughts of revenge. This is natural, but often plagues victims for years or a lifetime if there is no intervention. The crime continues to harm, because the victim continues the punishment by the inability to let go and move on with life. Every experience is tainted from then on. It is impossible to fully trust another when one is haunted by the past. Forgiveness is not for the perpetrator; it is a necessary step for the victim to recover personal power and peace. Victims of rape or childhood sexual abuse often refer to themselves as survivors. This is claiming the strength it took to have lived through it, and the next step is to move beyond and reclaim a life of wholeness and gratitude. Forgiveness does not mean forgetting, it means cutting the cord that binds and releasing into freedom.

Ho'oponopono

There is an ancient Hawaiian healing process called Ho'oponopono that has been used and passed on by many people. Morrnah Nalamaku Simeona (May 19, 1913 – February 11, 1992) is credited for teaching her version of Ho'oponopono, and bringing it into modern usage. Part of it is a repetition of a series of phrases. You simply repeat the phrases over and over, to no one in particular. It can also be done with a particular person in mind or during a tense situation. The premise behind it is that we are responsible for everything that happens. Even if we just hear about something, we become part of it. This is not meant to overwhelm us with guilt; rather it is with this understanding that we become free. It is the guilt from blaming that causes our suffering. Being self-responsible for everything around us empowers us to change our circumstances by changing ourselves. As we heal ourselves, we heal the world.

Experience Ho'oponopono for yourself.

- Sit in a relaxed, upright posture, and take a few deep breaths, letting them out slowly.

- Gaze for a moment at your heart and smile.

- Close your eyes and repeat these words: I'm sorry. I love you. Please forgive me. Thank you.

The great thing about Ho'oponopono is that it can be done anytime, anywhere, under any circumstances. All you have to do is remember it.

Chapter 2

PERCEPTION:
The WORLD IS *as*
WE SEE IT

Culture Colors
Our World

California Groov'n

*G*rowing up in the sixties and seventies in California, my perception of the world was greatly influenced by the hippies, the women's liberation movement, and rock and roll music, especially the Beatles. I was swaying to them in garage band dances when I was five. Then, on a trip to San Francisco during the summer of love in 1968, I was enthralled by all the wild and crazy flower children hippies tripping out in Haight Ashbury, the heart of the movement.

When I entered seventh grade, my favorite English teacher, the cool, mustached Mr. Raymond, had us writing poetry while listening to Crosby, Stills & Nash on the record player. I was writing and daydreaming about peace, love, and freedom. It was during that class that a friend and I conceived a plan to run away to Height Ashbury and become flower children. It was the early seventies by now, but we thought they would still be there.

I gave away all my treasured record albums, and many personal belongings to friends. Writing a farewell note, I thanked my parents for the great job they did raising me and told them I was ready to take it from there. My friend Julie and I got a ride from an older neighbor boy to the bus station in downtown San Diego. We bought our tickets and waited in the terminal for our departure.

As a policeman approached, we whispered to remember our alibis. A phone call later, to my primary grade school where I lied and said my mom taught, we were out to the patrol car and handcuffed to the metal grid dividing front and back. Not wanting to face our fate, we sang and laughed all the way to juvenile hall, and once there, practiced square dance steps on the grey linoleum floor. My father picked me up. He didn't say much, but he must have been hurt to the core, a probation officer having to bail his daughter out of juvenile hall. It was the only time I'd ever seen him cry. I never saw Julie again. Turns out, she was a chronic runaway, and was put in a home for troubled youth. I never tried it again.

By the eighties, a new cultural phenomenon arrived, Yuppies (young urban professionals). My hippie vision in the seventies was to someday have my grandparents' little yellow house with a trellis of sweet peas growing in front and to drive their Chevy Nova station wagon. I traded this in for the yuppie life, with my new older husband, Jim. We lived in a big house with an ocean view, in La Jolla, striving to make lots and lots of money in the beginning of my real estate career. I was only twenty-two. My first car purchase on my own was a big, sky-blue-Cadillac Eldorado. A must have in the business to secure the perception of myself and others of having success. How quickly my perceptions changed—and life changed as a result.

What remained with me from my teenage years was a strong value for independence and freedom. I chose a career where my earnings were tied to my own efforts (and learning the hard way early on—the shifting economy) rather than the dependable salary both my parents had. I think the adventurous, freedom loving, rebelliousness of the hippie culture served me well in striking a path on my own, as I became a broker as soon as the time limit allowed. I then opened my own office, working independently.

For myself, and many others, the anti-establishment perception that was fueled in part by anti-war demonstrations against our involvement in Vietnam, and disillusionment with the "shallowness" of capitalism became a full embrace of the establishment, and then carrying it farther, a perception took hold that the frenzied pursuit of material wealth was the way to achieve happiness and fulfillment. Our society experienced the result of that cultural shift, with corporate scandals and the financial meltdown of 2008. In recent years, amnesia about those events followed. The laws passed then, to protect the average investor and home buyer, one by one are being dismantled.

We are in the midst of another major cultural shift, and there are those, as usual, trying desperately to hold on to old ways of seeing and acting. The shifting sands of perception are always changing shape. The more we are firmly established in the Truth that never changes, and seeing reality as it is, the more resilient we are at accepting and thriving in a new world.

Another major influence that shaped my perceptions was women's liberation. My mother was a great role model. She was a career-woman and worked throughout my childhood, only taking a few years off, giving in to my sister's demands that she stay home. My father was very supportive of her teaching career, and, except for housework, they modeled a very equal relationship.

The marches and bra-burnings of the sixties led to some real headway for women to break into traditionally male careers. I was one of the recipients of all their efforts. My perception was that I could do anything a man could do, and I tried! I mowed the lawn, and my husband cooked. I went into commercial real estate, a male bastion to this day. I kept my own last name. I tried not to do anything "traditionally female." The one thing I never did, thankfully, was wear those little neckties with the blue business suits, that women thought they had to have to look successful and professional in the eighties.

I think the mistaken perception many women had, myself included, was that we judged success and happiness from a male point of view, trying so hard to be equal. We didn't realize then, that having equal rights did not mean having to live and act like a man. We can honor women's inherent talents, strengths, and differences, and begin to fully value women's work as much as we do men's. We can partner and collaborate with women, instead of perceiving them as competitors, as we often do. We can mentor young women and junior associates, encouraging their advancement. We can honor men, and their inherent strengths, talents, and differences, without having to act like them, or worse, blame them. Yet, with all the strides made in the last decades, we still have a ways to go. It begins with the way women and men perceive themselves, as men or women, as human beings—and the way we perceive and respect others.

Female or male, black, white, or brown, no matter what our particular differentiation is, and it is endless!, we can all move beyond the labels and connect with our own heart, and then reach out to others with love and respect.

We Create Our World

"We do not see the world as it is.
We see the world as we are."

For most of us, this quote is a truism. It may have come from the Talmud, or Anais Nin, depending on where you look. When we stand in our truth, it may be contrary to what others hold to be true. Our perception is colored by our age, geography, socialization, and culture that we were raised in and where we spend our time. It is influenced by where we place our attention, what we choose to read, watch, and expose ourselves to, our level of education, institution where we were educated, the political and economic climate of our time.

Perception is also created by how we see ourselves in relation to others and the world. Do I see myself as a worthy, valuable contributor? Do I view myself and others as basically good and trustworthy? Is the world full of beauty and intricate connection? Do I have personal power, or am I at the mercy of my circumstances? Am I responsible, or is the world to blame? Am I lovable? Are human beings part of the environment or rulers over it? Is it a dog-eat-dog world where there are only winners and losers? Does everything happen for a reason? Is there order, or is it just random chaos? Your answers to these and endless questions create your world.

In the modern world of the internet, we have access to so much information, but we have to have more and more discernment about what is constantly being directed our way. Arianna Huffington, in her book, *Thrive: The Third Metric to Redefining Success and Creating a Life of Well Being, Wisdom and Wonder* says,

> Increasingly, the world around us, or at least the one presented to us by the tool we choose to surround ourselves with, is designed—and very well at that—to take that element of surprise out of our path. The ever more sophisticated algorithms on the social media sites where we live our lives know what we like, so they just keep shoveling it to us. It's celebrated as "personalization," but it often caters to a very shriveled part of who we really are. They know what we like, but they don't know what we don't know we like—or what we need. They don't know our possibilities, let alone how vast they are.

The only way to know what you want or need is to come in from the outside and listen silently to the inner voice of truth. Most of us now have a permanent appendage called a cell phone. Every time it beeps with a call, text, or email, we've been programmed to think we have to know what it is about and respond immediately. For many, leaving our phone behind, for even a few minutes, feels akin to going without an arm. As a result, we've become rude to ourselves, people close to us, and business associates, taking calls and texting in the middle of or throughout conversations. We can't really be present for more than one thing; so we and whoever we are with are cut short.

Most of all, we hurt ourselves, by missing out on all of it. Research has shown that texting while driving is the same as driving drunk. Is the subreality of sound bites where you want to live? How objective is it when every response is instantaneous to something that is only partially taken in, and hasn't had time to be absorbed or reflected upon? In this plugged-in, accelerated world, we risk losing meaningful dialog, retrospection, and relationships. All becomes shallow, including us, unless we take time to unplug. Humans need time in natural environments to rest, relax, and recharge with the pure energy field that comes from trees, rocks, and the earth.

When we are connected with the natural energy field, we expand who we are. We touch again certain virtues and values that cross cultural, political, and religious boundaries, and that ring true for most. The words may not be the same, are couched differently in fables, myths, and proverbs, but the lesson and value we hold dear to our heart is the same. These are held, and passed through time in the collective consciousness.

"Many paths lead from the foot of the mountain, but at the peak we all gaze at the single bright moon." -Ikkyu

There is danger in being spoon fed only what we like. When we preach only to the choir, there is no one to challenge our assumptions. Those who live in an insular world tend to have a narrow sense of perception. I remember hearing the co-founder of The Omega Institute, Elizabeth Lesser, once say in a TED Talk, that she purposely seeks out those with opposing beliefs and agendas to her own and invites these individuals to have lunch with her. Unless we are exposed to the greater world, we believe that what we see and hear is the truth. We have no basis to believe differently. I have been blessed to travel extensively, but it was primarily in the United States and Europe—the Western view of reality. It wasn't until I began to study Eastern philosophy and spirituality that my mind was stretched to embrace other realities as true. When I traveled to India the first time, my mind and senses were blown wide open! It felt like entering an alternative world where the energy was accelerated. The sights, sounds, colors and smells were vibrant and intense. The smell of urine and strong incense, the towering skyscrapers shadowing over variegated metal shops with the family bedroom in back, maimed, begging children and brightly colored saris flying on the back of motorcycles, with two or three children wedged in between, blasting horns responding to the sign on all brightly painted work trucks: Honk please, so they would know when you want to pass.

The second time I flew into Mumbai, in 2007 when I would be staying for four months in an ashram in a small village about sixty miles away, I spent three days at the Hyatt in Mumbai to acclimate to the thirteen-hour time difference. Outside the window of my room, overlooking a community I later read about in the book, *Behind the Beautiful Forevers*, bright green birds that looked like parrots flew by my window. I had a bird's-eye view of people taking care of all their personal hygiene in the stream that ran alongside rows of shanties. The book gave a face and a glimpse into the lives I had overlooked, and yet having been in Mumbai added depth and meaning to the book.

It is good get shaken out of our complacency and have our senses shocked open once in awhile. It reminds us that there is more to this world than the narrow borders of our minds, that time and place impose. It awakens us into a new consciousness. Margaret Frings Keyes, in her book, *Out of the Shadows*, says,

Most of the world's work is done while we are functioning in ordinary consciousness, but a more objective awareness is possible. There is as much difference between objective consciousness and ordinary consciousness as there is between ordinary consciousness and sleep. In ordinary consciousness, we are not aware of inconsistencies and contradictions of our experience. For example, practically no one questions the peculiarities of a concept like "ownership." We seldom think of mysteries like suffering, death and life. We gloss over, or screen out, any data that does not support our Enneagram state.

Ordinary consciousness might be thought of as a semi-trance state into which we were induced by our culture in infancy. Our parents, our culture, our schooling, our "way of life", all reinforce its suggestions, so most of the time we exist in complete consensus with the people around us that this is the way things are. We glimpse this conditioning when we think of little enclaves "different from us" like fundamentalist Muslims, or urban slum children dealing drugs, or the mentally ill, but we do not see ourselves easily in this light.

Keyes says we gloss over or screen out any data that does not support our Enneagram state. The Enneagram is a system that maps out what drives us, what we are attracted to, and what we avoid. It reveals specific ways we color our perception. I will introduce the Enneagram in the next chapter.

Perception and the Three Centers of Intelligence

Relating to Our World

*I*t is helpful to have a map when you embark on a journey—
a map that will alert you to obstacles and detours, as well
as landmarks and spectacular views. Using GPS when driving,
we can filter for gas stations, coffee stops or hotels depending
on our needs. We can enter an exact location and be guided
there via the most expedient route. Our brain works much the
same way. Depending on our chief concerns, we will see the
world in a particular way. Areas of priority will be magnetized,
and everything else is minimized or missed altogether. This is
an efficient way of functioning. Millions of stimuli come at
us from all directions. Without a filtering system, we would
be overwhelmed. Learning which filter we are using helps to
discern when we get off track, and what we might be missing.
We normally think the brain is the center of intelligence, but
that is only one center. The heart has its own emotional intelligence, and the body intuits from what is often referred to as
the gut brain. Each center filters stimuli or experience from a
different set of priorities, which I will outline shortly. From my
research, I've found that the heart and gut intelligences travel
to different areas in the brain itself. The basics are that the
gut sends messages to the primitive, instinctual part of the

brain located at the brain stem, called the reptilian brain. The heart sends messages through the limbic system located in the midbrain, called the mammalian brain. The mental center of intelligence is the newest part of the brain, called the prefrontal cortex. We gravitate toward one as the dominant lens through which we perceive the world. Depending on which center is relied on most heavily is where our attention gets focused and priorities are formed.

Learning how I use and misuse the three centers of intelligence has helped me tremendously to grow in compassion, through understanding myself and others—and how we perceive the world in very different ways. It has assisted me in discerning and transforming the blocks that prevent me from connecting to my essential nature, my inner Self, which, I believe, is divine. Through shining a light on the cloudy filters that distort our perceptions, we begin to see ourselves more clearly and widen the scope of our vision, allowing us to perceive and understand the viewpoints of others. When we learn to access all three centers in a balanced way, the world of possibilities open wide. Awareness of and proficiency in balancing the centers of intelligence has wide application for developing greater emotional intelligence, communication, and presence, all components of a conscious leader. Although we need all three to survive—our head, heart, and body, we over depend on one center at the expense of the other two. Fully accessing mental, emotional, and body wisdom in a balanced way is integrated intelligence.

In fact, according to the Enneagram, which is an ancient system that delineates the centers and the way in which they become imbalanced, the personality is formed by their misuse.

Integrated intelligence is not about working to have a better personality, rather its purpose is to expose the false personality, and by coming into balance, revealing the authentic self. There are different ways we fall asleep to our essential qualities, the ones our soul child keeps tugging at us to remember and retrieve.

The Russian-Armenian mystic, Gurdjieff, who brought the Enneagram to the West, referred to this falling asleep as consensus trance. Our enculturation has created a trance-like existence where we react to life with defense mechanisms that we use unconsciously to survive in a world that requires conformance to the rules and standards of time, place, family, and society.

The outer layer, or ego, gets fixated on mental and emotional patterns, causing distortions in perception, and defense mechanisms arise in response, forming the personality. It is through forming this distorted filter we learned to cope with the lost connection with Essence, or the Knower, and which causes us to drift farther and farther away from our true nature. It is through this point that is also the path back to the wisdom of our inner self, and reconnection with Essence. Overdependence on one of the centers distorts what we experience. It is by recognizing the particular filters we use to formulate a limited point of view that we can begin to expand our perception in a global way.

There are three ways we most strongly relate to the world: through the body, also called the instinctual or gut center; through the head or mental center; or through the heart, or emotional center. There is an effective use for each center of intelligence, as well as overuse.

Those who are gut types, relate mainly through the body center of intelligence, kinesthetic sensations, and instincts. These individuals are most concerned with issues of autonomy and control: controlling others, and avoidance of being controlled, and control over one's environment. They are most focused on the basic need of worth. They are self-forgetting and outwardly focused. Anger is the dominant emotion, triggered by feelings of unworthiness.

Head types are influenced most by the mental center of intelligence and are most concerned with safety and security and are focused on a need for certainty. The meaning of life and our place in it is a focus. The primary emotion is fear in response to feeling uncertain and/or insecure. They plan, strategize worst case scenarios, and hide behind knowledge to avoid danger.

For those with a dominant emotional center of intelligence, the heart types are most concerned with creating an image and presentation to gain the approval of others. They are also concerned with how humans function in the world. The focus is on being loved, and the primary emotion is sadness, stemming from feeling they are not loved and cared about for who they really are.

While there are productive uses of each center, misuses happen when one or more of the centers of intelligence are out of balance: our attention and energy are focused on one center, and the others are ignored or inflamed. We misuse or overuse the dominant center, which skews the other two as well. The centers have a an effective use and misuse:

The functional uses for the body center are taking effective action, steadfastness, and gut knowing. The misuses are excessive action, passivity, and reactivity.

The productive uses of the mental center are objective analysis, astute insight, and productive planning. The misuses are overanalyzing, projection, and over-planning.

The productive uses of the heart center are empathy, authentic relating, and compassion. The misuses are emotional manipulation, playing roles, and oversensitivity.

When all three centers align, you are fully present and your authentic self shines through.

Three Centers of Intelligence

BODY CENTER
Sensations: Gut
Anger and Control

HEAD CENTER
Mental: Thoughts
Fear and Doubt

HEART CENTER
Emotions: Feelings
Distress and
Neediness

PRESENCE
Authentic Self

Integration: The Centers of Intelligence

We need all three centers of intelligence, mental, emotional, and physical working in harmony in order to feel centered and calm. This allows us to act capably and accomplish what we need to effectively. We begin to function at a higher capacity and act consciously through our essential qualities rather than unconsciously reacting using our defense mechanisms. Out of balance means out of presence. When heart, mind and body are out of sync, we are somewhere besides here and now—dwelling in the past, projecting into the future, lost in emotions, or stuck in trying to control. When all three are in sync, we are aware of and accepting reality as it is, without a distorted spin. We have access to objective reality, and become a witness to ordinary reality, rather than under its spell. By revealing our dominant center, and underlying patterns of thinking, feeling and acting, the Enneagram gets deep to the heart of it. It is one of the most effective systems out there for building emotional intelligence.

The mental center searches for certainty in its need for security, safety and protection to overcome fear. Clarity and wisdom, visioning a bright future and being awake and prepared are gifts of Enneagram head center types. The essential qualities of the mental center are awareness, or inner knowing, a quiet, peaceful mind, and listening to and trusting inner guidance. We can think calmly and rationally, and realistically assess the situation at hand, without bias or projection of our own fears. Our actions are informed by knowing and are intentional.

When our feeling center is used in an integrated way, we know our true value, we know who we really are, and we relate to others authentically with genuine feeling. We are in touch with the depth of our feelings and can feel them fully and express them to others. There is no hidden agenda. We are neither over-sensitive nor calloused, and our feelings and reactions are appropriate to the situation at hand.

Integrated or distorted centers create the inner landscape. Our inner state affects the way we view reality, and how we communicate with others, on all levels. Just think about the last time you stepped into a room where two people were arguing; the sensation is palpable.

The body's intelligence comes from the gut brain. Neuroscience research is finding the validity and important functions of the gut brain. Whether or not we treat our body in an integrated way affects our point of reference. What we ingest weighs in on perception. Weighted down with junk food, or processed, salty frozen entrees, or sugary drinks, a sort of brain-fog descends, clouding clear perception. Eating whole, fresh, natural foods, and minimal sugar and caffeine intake clears the mind and balances the emotions. Some recommend a fast at the change of each season to rebalance the system and increase clarity. This reminds me of an old saying, "We are what we eat."

Emotions play a role in making the world a terrifying hell, a monotonous blur, or an exciting adventure. Emotional intelligence (EQ) has been found to have a greater influence on success and satisfaction with career and life than IQ. It doesn't matter how smart you are, if your emotions are out of control, your world will be topsy-turvy. A part of EQ is reactivity. The higher the level of EQ, the lower the reactivity. Learning to pause, breathe deeply, count to ten are ways to self regulate. We can't control what happens to us, only how we respond. It's the story we tell our self in the midst of an event and after that determines our future. In fact, it's the stories we make up that determine reality.

Test it out. When you are in the middle of an uncomfortable situation, pause, notice your breath, and then watch your mind. What are the stories playing? The mind fits past situations into the current box and makes a judgment of good or bad, pleasant or unpleasant. Instead of going down that slippery slope, feel the emotions that arise in reaction to the story and judgment. Acknowledge the feelings without trying to change them. Where do you feel them? What are the body sensations? The trained mind of an emotionally intelligent person also asks, is it pleasurable or beneficial? And then he or she chooses the beneficial. This is the moment of choice: stick to the old story and react accordingly; or ride through the discomfort, let go of the judgment and take appropriate action to the current situation. This rewrites the story.

As Don Riso and Russ Hudson explained in *Wisdom of the Enneagram*, having full use of the body center means being grounded through experiencing the world through our senses, and having a gut knowing about what is real. We are present in the moment, where our feet are. Our breath is full and our attention is focused on now. We are aware of our body and the environment in which we find ourselves. We take right action in the right moment.

There is a common tendency to lose touch with the dominant center, yet be unaware of being driven by that center. As we saw above, there is an effective use of each center, and there is an ineffective use that happens when we perceive and act relying heavily on one center, so that information from the other two centers either fade into the background and don't have much influence, or are blown out of proportion by the pressure from the dominant center.

Optimally, we want to be high functioning at all times, but this is most often not the case. This is because the three centers are not fully integrated, creating a distorted filter of perception that causes us to react in inappropriate ways. As long as we skew reality through an imbalance in the centers of intelligence, our filter remains distorted. How do we achieve integration? By becoming self-aware and fully present in our body, noticing sensations, so that we have full access to all three centers at once. Meditation, slow deep breathing, and conscious body movement are excellent ways to integrate. Stillness, being in nature, and focusing on our heart, allowing it to open, are also excellent ways of gaining equanimity.

Without developing awareness of our imbalances, and the skill to come into equanimity, we remain below an optimum level of emotional intelligence (EQ). High levels of emotional and social intelligence are achieved by developing self-mastery. Self-mastery means that one is aware of one's own thoughts, emotions, and actions and is able to witness these as an observer. This enables the ability to catch oneself in the act, or preferably, before acting. Then it's easier to decide what is most appropriate in the moment. Without this ability to be self-aware and observant, habitual patterns of thinking, feeling, and acting take over and react with defense mechanisms that are largely unconscious and automatic.

When there is even a moderate level of self-mastery, one begins to be proactive rather than reactive. The more proficiency in self-awareness, the greater the power of choice one has. This is true freedom. One of my favorite quotes, sums up the reason to study oneself through a lens like the Enneagram. It is from Viktor E. Frankl, an Austrian psychologist who was a holocaust survivor. He says in his book *Man's Search for Meaning*: "When we are no longer able to change a situation, we are challenged to change ourselves."

Changing ourselves is impossible without self-awareness. Changing ourselves and our perception of the world and our circumstances is the only true power we have. For when we change, the world around us changes. Making a positive difference in the world starts by living and embodying higher beliefs and virtues. If we don't see and feel the underlying harmony of the universe, or have faith and hope in ourselves and humankind, then there is no real possibility of change. Without inner knowing, we cannot envision a better world. Without the love and joyfulness of our shared origin and oneness, there's no real and lasting commitment.

For instance, social and environmental activism doesn't carry much weight or effect real change until the consciousness of people and society changes. The deep work of activism and facilitating major change is the inner transformation of the activists and change agents themselves. Commitment to inner work leads the way to personal and social responsibility, without which any movement remains a blame game, reinforcing existing polarities and the current state of affairs. This was the call of Gandhi to his fellow Indian citizens oppressed by British rule for a few centuries: "If we could change ourselves, the tendencies in the world would also change. As a man changes his own nature, so does the attitude of the world change towards him…"

Not only do we change our self and our view of the world when we experience inner transformation, but the attitude of others towards us also changes. When we feel confidence, others have confidence in us. When we trust our self, we become trustworthy.

The Body Center of Intelligence

*T*here is movement, even in stillness. Blood is circulating, breath flows, inside and outside. When movement ceases, we cease to exist. Even the soul travels to its next destination. The body gives a sense of grounding, and place in the world. Fully inhabiting the body center in a conscious way is presence. Knowing where you are, your surroundings, the sensations you are experiencing, skin deep and inside. Whether the neck and shoulders are relaxed, the stomach muscles are constricted, what is happening in the moment, inside and outside. A big part of the body consists of internal systems that run on their own, circulation and digestion, for instance. We can tune in to those systems too. One of my favorite reminders to return to presence is, *be where your body is*. Chances are, if you've lost body awareness, you are somewhere else.

The body center is the place of action. The body takes thoughts and feelings and translates them into doing something. Gut level reactions cause instantaneous movement—retreat, advance, expand or contract. The mind catches up later. Somatic awareness is the practice of body awareness; soma is a Greek derived word meaning body. Body awareness includes sensations, as well as thoughts and feelings; where they are located in the body and how the body responds.

What better way to return to presence than movement? Wiggle, sway. tap, pat, squat, lift, resist, expand. Any of those can be performed while standing in place. Amy Cuddy and Twyla Tharp (she had a new book out in 2019 called *Keep it Moving: Lessons For the Rest of Your Life*) both talk about the importance of taking up more space. Stand and walk boldly, while lengthening your stride. Doing this helps us to speak out with confidence. Confidence requires presence. Only when fully occupying the body does confidence arise. Inhabiting our body, being comfortable in our own skin, allows us to fully engage with life. When there is dissatisfaction with the body, often, there is dissatisfaction with life. We miss out on opportunities that are right in front of us.

Confidence is the elixir that causes people to look up from their smart devices and pay attention. When you exude confidence, you maintain eye contact, lean in to listen, and speak with authority. Your body is expanded, open and aligned All this gets you noticed and taken seriously. If you are paying attention, you may have noticed that all of these are actions.

Confidence, when ungrounded comes off as arrogance. The body center is home to presence, steadfastness and gut knowing, all necessary for true confidence.

The body is home to congruency. The body does not lie. You can fake affectations and you can speak an untruth, but the body reveals what's really going on. Yes, you can assume a stance to underscore the image you want to portray, but either the thoughts and emotions will shift to match the stance, or eventually the body will revert to its truth. The imprint of natural tendencies, attunement, environment and culture combine to create a unique way we each inhabit our body. Richard

Strozzi Heckler, who some refer to as the father of somatic coaching, said in his book, *The Art of Somatic Coaching:*

> Choice follows awareness. The more aware we are, the more choice we have. Cultivating awareness is the cornerstone to an awakened, robust life. Somatic awareness brings increased choice in our actions, moods, thoughts, feelings and way of being....The first step in Somatic Awareness is becoming aware of our sensations. Sensations are the building blocks of life and the foundational language of life. Sensations appear as temperature, pressure, shape and movement. They are sources of information and a direct way of connecting with the self. Sensations are always present and they are interlinked with our thinking, acting, feeling, sensing,perception and emotions. By bringing our attention to sensations, we can bring ourselves into the present moment.

The more we trust our gut, the greater is our ability to take resolute action. How connected to your body and its wisdom are you? Those that are confident tend to listen to and follow their gut instinct. As one who leads with the head center, when my thoughts run away with me, I lose the precious wisdom of my body and clarity of mind. The quickest way back to center is to go on a walk and feel myself moving on the ground. If I can connect my feet directly to the earth, dirt, sand or grass, even better. I breathe fresh air deeply into my belly, and before long my mind is quiet, my emotions have calmed, and I am present to the beauty that surrounds me. I'm more in touch with sensations, and can tune in to the messages I'm receiving from them. I finish with renewed focus, calmness and energy.

Confidence is a deep knowing that we are worthy. Confidence is a quality that emanates from within; it is in our bones. When we know our true worth and what we stand for, confidence arises, enabling us to speak our truth with clarity and conviction.

Many times sensations are ignored, thought of as distractions or nuisances, yet they are actually the gateway into presence. Getting to know the language of sensations gives us greater power over the quality of our life, and even the world around us.

Action Step:

Yoga poses are a great way to access the body's wisdom and return to presence. Mountain Pose is particularly effective, and can be done anywhere, anytime, even in a crowd:

- Stand and bring feet hip width apart, and align hips over feet. Elongate your spine up through the crown of the head, and lower and widen your shoulders.

- Relax your neck. Feel your weight evenly distributed on the balls and back of your feet, as well as the sides of your feet.

- You can rock slightly forward and back, side to side to balance and feel the center point. Inhale and exhale and feel your breath moving throughout your body, and imagine inhaling all the way though to the earth, and exhaling the breath all the way back up through the spine out the crown of the head.

- Gaze softly ahead, eyes slightly lowered and unfocused. Stay here as long as you like, noticing with nonjudgment, sensations, openings or constrictions, thoughts or emotions arising.

- Feel confidence shining through? Make Mountain Pose a daily practice and watch what happens.

Three Basic Instincts

Red Alert: Do You Know Who's Driving Your Bus?

As I waited for results of an MRI scan, I reviewed the last years. It was early 2015 when my mammogram came back suspicious. A biopsy revealed early stage breast cancer, and my world was turned upside down. My response was to keep moving. I wanted to share my story in the spirit of service, so I posted an article on LinkedIn titled, "When the Truth Is Hard to Face," and received an outpouring of support. My reaching out with vulnerability prompted countless personal sharing of stories about experiences with breast or prostate cancer, their own or loved ones. I was honored to listen, and was inspired by the strength and resilience of everyone involved in the journey, both the patient and the loved ones alongside. In turn, it strengthened my resolve to stay positive.

When we have a scare, our instincts kick in. Our instinctual nature is a part of us that is largely subconscious. The instincts do their work without us orchestrating—reacting automatically for our own good and sometimes, turns out, it's not so beneficial. What may be surprising is that our instinctual nature is calling the shots more often than we realize.

Each of the instincts has its own agenda. The survival instinct, is primary among three basic instincts, self preservation (safety, security, comfort), sexual (energy and procreation), and social (social bonding, belonging and status in a group or community). When a life threatening diagnosis comes, or when confronted with a dangerous situation, everything else becomes secondary. Survival goes straight to the top of the priority list. Let's get this taken care of now! The other two instincts can assist. The social instinct promotes involvement with work and community, and connection to colleagues and friends, which are crucial to the healing process. The sexual or one to one instinct provides energy to maintain the sparkle and enthusiasm in life, and love and support from our intimate partner and closest friends, all of which can work miracles in extending quality of life and even lifespan.

We tend to favor, or over use one instinct at the detriment of one or both of the others. When confronted with a crisis, it brings home the necessity of having full awareness of all three and the ability to use them in a balanced way. Most of us never think about our instinctual nature, and it continues to operate without our awareness or intervention. When we bring conscious awareness to this underlying motivational system, and discern which one we favor most, we begin to see what drives us.

A common analogy to determine your primary instinct is to imagine arriving at a party. Upon entering, if your first priority is to find the drinks and food, see if the temperature is right, and find a comfortable chair, you may be a self preservation subtype in Enneagram terms.

If you immediately scan the room to see whose energy you are most drawn, and pursue a conversation with that person, you may be a sexual or one to one subtype.

If you are relishing an evening among your community of

friends and fellow enthusiasts, or concerned about your status in the group, you may rely most on your social instinct.

This is helpful to know, because it not only shades the personality in a particular way, your perception of the world is also colored by what your primary focus is. The way in which we perceive something has huge implications on the quality of and ability to succeed in life. Ideally, we will take care of our need to be safe, healthy, enthusiastic and connected, and part of a supportive group or community in a skillful and balanced way.

The more aware we become of which aspects we are blind to, which hum along without much thought, and which one can make us feel obsessed, the greater our chances are of developing a well rounded team of high functioning instincts to facilitate positive change. If you are handicapped in one or all the instincts, life's challenges can be difficult to overcome.

During two rounds of breast cancer, I was challenged to use all three instincts at peak levels. My spiritual community and friends brought meals as I recovered from surgery. I'm not one to easily ask for help, but I followed a friend's suggestion and signed up at a website that sends invites to a list of friends with appropriate food and dates to sign up. I took the time off needed to heal, and I exercised, slept and read myself to recovery.

Immediately after the first mastectomy, I met someone and had the courage to be vulnerable and risk a new relationship. We met ten days after surgery, and I was still bandaged and recovering. I told him about it, and gave him an easy out if it made him uncomfortable. He assured me he was fine with it, and the sweet energy of a budding romance enlivened every cell in my body, contributing greatly to healing. Although I'm sure he wondered about the bad luck of another cancer diagnosis a year later, and if I would ever be strong and healthy, he stuck with me. He was my angel, there for me through five surgeries, each time accompanying me to the hospital and offering his home for recovery.

I am immensely grateful for so many things. I am aware and accepting of my instinctual nature, and gently adjust when I catch myself out of alignment. The MRI came out fine, and I am strong and healthy! I have a tight knit group of friends and fellow travelers on the path of meditation, which enrich me in so many ways. I love my work and am beginning again to expand and thrive with new clients and renewed enthusiasm and commitment. I have a healthy relationship that is easeful, supportive, loving and fun.

Our Instinctual Nature

Within the body center lie the instincts. Instincts are part of what is often called the reptilian brain, where the fight, flight, or response happens. We are all motivated by our instinctual nature. There are three primary instinctual drives that we respond to in an automatic way, without conscious thought. They influence the way we perceive and act in the world, and each of us has a dominant focus of action on one, creating a distorted view, or bias, according to the Enneagram experts. The preoccupation with one of the instincts colors our personality and perspective.

These three instincts are: self-preservation, which is survival and sustenance; social, having to do with power and place in the group; and sexual, which is concerned with energy, intimate relationships, and our need to be in tune and connected with others. The core fear for all of us is fear for our survival and well being, and so that fear gets filtered through the other two instincts, as well. For instance, if you are dominated by the sexual instinct, it may feel like you are going to die if you do not have a romantic relationship. If you are social dominant, you live as if survival depends on your standing in the group. Whatever our primary instinct is, this is the area of life where our habitual patterns and passions play out most dramatically. It is where we expend the greatest effort, and are most preoccupied. Becoming self-aware of our dominant drive and observing how it runs the show can be a major catalyst for transformation and greater success in life. What separates humans from other mammals is our higher center of thought, which is the executive function of the brain, located in the prefrontal cortex. This gives humans power over our instinctual nature through discernment. In the space of a pause, an intake of breath, humans can intervene on their own behalf and change course. It is also here, in the newest part of the brain, unique to our species, that we form beliefs, have intuition, and expand beyond individual knowing into higher intelligence or connection with universal knowing. I find it fascinating that the third eye, between and just above the eyebrows, talked about by the ancients as the place of intuition, is where the prefrontal cortex is, at the front of the forehead. Arianna Huffington, in *The Fourth Instinct: The Call of the Soul,* talks about the fourth instinct as a connection to our soul's highest knowing that brings us out of our base nature full of competition and survival of the fittest, to cooperation and collaboration, and survival of the wisest.

Huffington describes the influence of each of the three primary instincts on us as human beings. On the survival instinct, she says:

> Armed with an automatic biological reflex to counter physical danger, it is here to insure that we keep body and soul together... But more often, wherever we live, it is perceived dangers that primarily trigger the survival instinct—the adrenal rush before we ask for a raise, or the clammy hands before we ask for a date. It may be a false alarm, but it trips a flood of anxiety that is no less

real than if we confronted a mugger in a dark, deserted street. It is a reaction that runs counter to all the animating impulses of our Fourth Instinct, trust, acceptance and the peace that passes all understanding. Worry is a form of atheism. And so is most fear.

Those last two sentences caught my attention. That is a blunt statement. As a fear type, one who perceives from the mental center, I can get caught up in worry. It's not a pleasant concept to grasp, but I have to agree. In those moments when worry or fear plague me, my inner connection with God is not present, or at least not felt. That is why it has been vitally important to develop daily practices that have become habitual, so I can find my way back to trust, peace and acceptance. When I meditate, I reconnect with something greater than myself and it restores equanimity. Most of what I worry about never comes to pass, it only serves to keep me from presence. Presence is the only place of agency, where I can exercise choice and have power over what happens.

Huffington has this to say about the social instinct:

> The second instinct is Nietzsche's will to power...It is the instinct by which we choose our options in the world, make plans, execute them, and commit ourselves to a life of action. Here is self-assertion, the drive to assert ourselves as a force with which creation will need to reckon. Without the push of our second instinct, we might still be making mud pies in the sun. Under its stern guidance, we have conquered the world. We have shed the light of reason on it, but we have missed both the source of a greater light, and what the dark corners have to teach. We have mastered nature, but in the process we have cut ourselves off from nature's master plan.

She says about the sexual instinct,

Whether thwarted or fulfilled, this is a drive that can
defy and overwhelm man's reason with glory or terror...
The ancients recognized the ambivalent power of our
sexual instinct—a tidal wave beneath which we drown
or on which we ride into a life lived more intensely, more
truthfully, more consciously.

No matter what the domain, our life will be primarily
influenced by our dominant instinct. For instance, with social
dominant personalities, rejection by a group may feel like their
very survival is threatened.

When our instinctual nature is in sync, life hums along
smoothly. Ups and downs, challenges and victories, loves and
losses are experienced and managed skillfully. Body, mind and
heart are fully present and engaged. We have greater access to
and ability to listen and follow our deepest wisdom. We are
resilient and able to adapt quickly to change. As conscious
leaders, we lead ourselves first. Then others follow our example.

The following poems express my experience of these instinctual energies that surface, disturbing the calm of day, and the
slumber of late night.

The Massive Tree of Rage

The massive tree overwhelms the forest.
Branches spread everywhere, stealing the light
from struggling saplings below.
It's thick, grasping roots suck molten lava
from the ancient depths of earth.

Gnarled trunk rising up, contorted by years of seething,
Even the woodpecker no longer seeks to penetrate.
This loud, blustering exterior hides a stark truth
within thousands of bark beetles feast,
eating ring upon ring of dark edged
memory of forests raped.

Dark, craggy bark, defending only emptiness.
Just waiting for lightening to strike
And end this hell.

Adrenaline Alarm

Awakening in the pre-dawn hours,
fearing what life will bring.
My heart gripped with anxiety, will I survive?
What's around the corner?
Who am I that life is so good?
Will it come crashing in and disappear?
The late-night phone rings the death bell;
the bogey man is here!

Deep inhalations give no relief.
Turning on the light, I reach for poet saints
to comfort me,
Expanding my horizons, as they revel in ecstasy.
My little life and big fears become
Meaningless in the greater scheme of things.

Just put on a hat and
Dance with the moon.
Fly free skipping across the clouds.
Up here the air is clear, unsoiled by debris.
Looking down upon mindless clutter
Its only particles of dust!

Tickle a cloud until its laughter bursts raindrops
Dissolving into the sea.
Paddling through life riding the waves
Feeling the spray in my face.
Scared wordless at the top of the crest,
Crashing down for a mouthful of sand.
Bursting out to a breath of fresh air.

All is calm again,
Let's go back to sleep.

Action Step:

- Are you feeling out of balance?
  Like someone else is driving your bus?

- Check in with your three primary instincts.

- Sit quietly and tune inside.

- Notice sensations in your body.

- As Enneagram teacher, Jessica Dibbs says, "the instincts
  are seated in the body, in the first three chakras, or
  energy centers; first-root at the sacrum, second-lower
  belly, and third-solar plexus, self preservation, one on
  one, and social, respectively."

- Breathe into these places along the spinal column.

- What feelings arise?

- Where are your thoughts? Stay aware of sensations in any part of the body. It helps to journal whatever comes up, without judgment.

- What's working in your life?

- Where are you having problems?

- Which instinct has domain over any issue or problem that arises in your consciousness?

The Heart Center of Intelligence

"How does one know if she has forgiven? You tend to feel sorrow over the circumstance instead of rage, you tend to feel sorry for the person rather than angry with him. You tend to have nothing left to say about it all." ~CLARISSA PINKOLA ESTÉS

For much of my life, I was afraid to stand up and speak my truth, especially if someone was aggressively pressuring me to do something. I was afraid of incurring their wrath, or disfavor, and was fearful of hurting others feelings. I would agree, but then I would seethe after. One of the typical ways I reacted was to withdraw. I would disappear in a book, or leave and go somewhere. In romantic relationships, each time it happened, I would withdraw a little more of myself until a wall formed that was an emotional barrier. What I didn't realize was that wall was not just impermeable to negative emotions, but to positive ones as well. Eventually, I just felt numb. One boyfriend called me an ice queen, and unfortunately that's how I felt. I even had dreams after that relationship ended that I was in an ice cave. Following is the story of the most unhealthy, damaging relationship of my life. It caused me to question my ability to judge people's character accurately.

Tough Lessons

*H*ow could a strong, confident young business woman who had owned her own company be taken in by a fraud and allow a takeover of her life? Shame. Unhealed shame is devastating. It will take you into the gutter like nothing else can.

He was so smooth, brilliant in a twisted sort of way. I kept the illusion that I was in control. I drove when we went places together, and I made the money. He needed me to always be there for him to help ease the pain of the nerve damage in his leg. All the while, he was performing a calculated brainwashing.

I bought his story, as did many others, my friends and his. He said he had a Thanatologist PhD, a psychologist specializing in death, dying, and grieving who had played college football as #62 for the Oklahoma Sooners. He was on disability for a work-related injury. There was a tiny thread of truth to his stories from which he built his identity, which was why they didn't draw more questions.

His portrayal of being a psychologist led me to believe him when he said that it wasn't healthy for a relationship to spend time apart. I thought my marriage was proof of that. I couldn't be trusted. We spent twenty-four hours a day together. I remember just wanting so bad sometimes just to go to the store by myself. Before long, he was even going to work with me, and attending meetings with clients, as my personal sales trainer. We gave him a bogus title of "Research and Development."

My whole life was now saying "yes" to a master manipulator, when my soul was crying for me to say "No!" But I couldn't admit to myself or anyone else that I was so wrong in the choice I'd made. He smoothed my losses by taking me to open houses in coastal neighborhoods every weekend, telling me a former business associate would arrange a no down, low interest loan for him. All top secret, of course.

I relocated my business to the Palm Springs area with a local company, and in just over a year was able to purchase a new home with a pool in the backyard. I had the down payment and qualified for the loan by myself, but his name went on the title. I just knew I couldn't have done it without his help.

This man was a rager—yelling, blaming, and demanding right in my face. He controlled me through my fear of his rage and my sympathy for his physical pain. He was smart enough to know the limit of my tolerance, and he never crossed the line into physical abuse. Even though he never hit me, my heart and self-confidence were beat to shreds. He controlled my physical space by always being in it and my time by watching it like a hawk. The times I managed to go somewhere by myself, if I wasn't back the minute I said I'd be, I'd incur his wrath. One day, when I arrived a half hour late, he threw a phone across the room.

One place he couldn't penetrate was the ladies locker room at the popular health club we belonged to at one of the country clubs. After a workout and shower one evening, I was changing next to a client's wife, and casually asked where she was headed.

She answered Al-Anon. My curiosity peaked—what's that? She explained that it was a twelve-step program for families and friends of alcoholics, and invited me to a meeting. I went, and she became my sponsor for the next fifteen years.

I attended weekly meetings down in the basement of a local hospital. On one night, a woman was going to the Co-dependents Anonymous meeting on another floor. I followed her, and as the description of a codependent was read, it hit me straight on—that's ME! By the time I started Al-Anon, our relationship had soured, so his grip loosened. He was spending long weekends in San Diego, and started another relationship with a woman at the gym. I finally had the courage to end it, but he continued living in the master bedroom while I moved to the guest room! A few months later, he moved out, leaving all his things, both car payments, high credit card balances and a threat to sue me for palimony.

Shattered, it was 1991, the beginning of a deep recession, which reinforced the illusion that I couldn't be successful without him. It took a year to trade the house for a condo. I told myself I'd keep his things for another year. When he didn't come for them, I gave away his clothes and returned an antique school desk he'd taken to his first wife. Going through his boxes and talking to both his former wives, I pieced together the real story behind the man I thought I knew. This process and therapy slowly deprogrammed the brainwashing. It took me years to trust my instincts and judgment again, and regain confidence in my abilities. An Al-Anon staple, the Serenity Prayer, was a constant companion, *God, grant me the serenity to accept the things I cannot change, the courage to change the things I can, and the wisdom to know the difference.* I'm eternally grateful to my parents for helping me through those rough years. I'll never forget my dad gave me a book called *Love and Money*, which I never read. I had to learn the hard way.

This poem speaks for itself!

Suspended in Ice

Words pop up, stinging like shots from a BB gun.
Too strong, too slow, too hard, too weak,
too cold, like an ice queen.
Every jab, another layer freezes over.

Too strong, too slow, too hard, too weak;
until I'm so numb I can't feel a thing.
every jab another layer freezes over;
this frozen field longs for spring.

Until I'm so numb I can't feel a thing,
staying as if suspended in ice.
This frozen field longs for spring,
for flower shoots and warm muzzles.

Staying as if suspended in ice,
frozen solid with fear of being alone.
For flower shoots and warm muzzles,
take a chance with a meltdown.

Frozen solid with fear of being alone,
a man's wounds become my own.

Take a chance with a meltdown;
please burn away all that's not mine.

A man's wounds become my own,
through a misguided notion of love.
Please burn away all that's not mine,
as words pop up stinging like shots from a BB gun.

Passions and Virtues

"Be wild; that is how to clear the river. The river does not flow in polluted, we manage that. The river does not dry up, we block it. If we want to allow it its freedom, we have to allow our ideational lives to be let loose, to stream, letting anything come, initially censoring nothing. That is creative life. It is made up of divine paradox. To create one must be willing to be stone stupid, to sit upon a throne on top of a jackass and spill rubies from one's mouth. Then the river will flow, then we can stand in the stream of it raining down." ~CLARISSA PINKOLA ESTÉS,

When you experience negative emotions such as fear, jealousy, confusion, just allow whatever is there, without judgment. Take a time-out to check in with the great-heart, by breathing slowly and deeply. As you do this, call forth the virtues that would be most helpful in the moment, such as strength, courage, or kindness, and just breath it in, allowing disturbing emotions to release with the exhale. It can be helpful to think of a pleasant experience, of all the things in your life that you are grateful for. Studies in Emotional Intelligence have shown that dwelling on the situation or person that brought up the emotion, just fuels the fire and escalates the uncomfortable feelings. There is a balance to be struck between noticing and acknowledging the feelings, and escalating them and getting stuck. The passions are anger, pride, deceit, envy, avarice, fear, gluttony, and lust. Through using our centers in a balanced way, the passions are transformed into virtues: serenity, humility, truthfulness, equanimity/balance, nonattachment, courage, sobriety, innocence, and right action. The more balanced we become, the more the virtues lead our lives and our inner sense of being.

In the foreword to Sandra Maitri's book, *Passions and Virtues*, A.A. Almaas said, "The virtues are the expression of the openness and development of the heart due to the realization of spiritual nature from inner transformation." The greater our heart connection, the more powerful is our inner transformation. In fact, transformation is not possible without the heart's participation. Without a meaningful heart connection, we are simply ruled by our ego, negative emotions, and passions. Communicating heart to heart are the virtues in action.

We see ourselves in relation to others through the lens of both passions and virtues, and it colors how we then relate to others. Sandra Maitri, says, "This basic sense of self and other is not usually conscious, nor is the passion, and it takes a good deal of inner work to expose it."

It is through self-observation that we begin to see our inner workings, and therefore develop choices in the way we relate to ourselves and others. When we are unaware, our ego is in control, and we operate mostly from the passions, or negative emotions. The more self-aware we become, the less the ego has a hold on us, and the virtues, or positive emotions begin to shine through and direct our actions and our life.

From pain, great creativity can emerge to process the agony and move through it to a transformed state and self. Without creative outlet, the wound will fester and grow. This poem is one example of the movement toward acceptance and equanimity.

Daily Openings

When he leaves without saying where,
when he hangs up with no "I love you,"
when his words are harsh or abrupt,

my mind races to dire conclusions,
my emotions turn toward anger,
my heart fastens one more chain.

When I follow my breath,
when I focus on the Name,
when I turn my gaze inside,

my mind watches thoughts scatter,
my emotions swirl in a tranquil pool,
my heart breaks another lock.

I am here to know what I cannot see.
I am here to reach beyond my skin,
to long for Oneness in many forms.

Emotional Presence

"When you are sorrowful look again in your heart,
and you shall see that in truth you are weeping
for that which has been your delight.
Some of you say, "Joy is greater than sorrow,"
and others say, "Nay, sorrow is the greater."
But I say unto you, they are inseparable.
Together they come,
and when one sits alone with you at your board,
remember that the other is asleep upon your bed.
Verily you are suspended like scales
between your sorrow and your joy."

— KHALIL GIBRAN, AUTHOR OF *The Prophet*

Sometimes we can't name what we are feeling. When we can name it, we own it, and can let it just be. Being mindful of what sensations are happening in the body, feelings that are arising and the running commentary of thoughts brings us into the present moment, where life is happening. Awareness of surroundings—the feel of temperature, air touching the skin, sights, smells, and sounds, brings us out of the daydream and into now. I appreciate the saying, *be where your feet are*. When we connect with the earth, by feeling our feet firmly planted, the energy that was stuck in our head, monopolized, fills our entire body.

Eckart Tolle, in *A New Earth: Awakening to Your Life's Purpose* described a moment of transformation for a woman, when he simply asked her to be with her feelings:

> At this moment, this is what you feel, there is nothing you can do about the fact that at this moment this is what you feel. Now, instead of wanting this moment to be different from the way it is, which adds more pain to the pain that is already there, is it possible for you to completely accept that this is what you feel right now?

There are so many messages running through our head about what we should and should not feel, including positive attitude advice, that most of the time we don't give ourselves permission to just be with whatever is there, without judgment. Feelings aren't permanent; in fact, they are hard to intentionally hold on to. Have you ever allowed yourself a good cry, full-out with no restrictions? How long does it last? The same with a good laugh. There is only so much, until it runs its course, and then we shift to something else. It is when we deny or suppress feelings that they overcome us, and feel unwieldy. When we are in a depression that doesn't lift, that indicates we need to seek the help of professionals.

Emotions have been likened to a bee landing on different petals of a lotus flower. When our mind alights on the petal of anger, anger arises, then it flits to sadness, elation, then back to anger. It doesn't stay in one spot for long. Our emotions play a continual song with endless patterns of variation and repetition. Emotions arise as memories are triggered by a favorite piece of music, a particular chord, a fragrance or the smell of food wafting from a doorway. In fact, our olfactory glands can elicit very powerful memories.

Noticing our repetitive thoughts and feelings gives us clues to which center of intelligence we are most identified. If angry thoughts of injustice, control or retribution play out on our inner screen most frequently, then we may identify most with the body center, and gut instincts. If anxiety wakes us up in the night regularly, with feelings of fear, worry, and insecurity, we may live in the mental center dominantly. Once we know where we are at, we can enlist the help the other centers to calm us and bring a return to equilibrium, such as taking a brisk walk to calm the agitated mind. Then we can be more objective, and less identified with our emotional state. Acting from a state of equanimity has a way of transforming difficult circumstances and relationships. When we shift, everything shifts, for we are not an isolated island.

In her book, *Emotional Alchemy: How the Mind Can Heal the Heart,* Tera Bennett-Goleman says,

> If we don't move beyond our personal identification with our own pain or confusion, we can miss another opportunity. We need to be open to deeper insights that might redefine our limited sense of ourselves, or of others. If we get too caught up in grappling with our emotions, we might miss the chance to turn toward essential qualities within. We might miss significant messages from the very pain we have been resisting. Or we might begin to identify too much with our patterns rather than releasing them. Release would allow us to free up energy that had been trapped, letting us be more creative, more present, more available—or of greater service—to others.

The heart center of intelligence is all about connection. How connected do you feel to those around you, not just your closest family and friends, but to the people you work with and lead? How much do you reveal to them about yourself, and how curious are you about their thoughts, feelings and lives? In an era of technology and social media, real time, face to face interaction has become a rarity, and loneliness and shallow interaction has become the norm. The ability to deeply connect with self and others has become elusive, yet it is a primary quality of presence.

Another way the heart center is involved in connection, is through an energy from the heart that connects us to others. Coherence is described as clarity and understanding and that helps connection, when others are clear about who you are and what you stand for. There's also something larger going on, called Social Coherence, researched by Heart Math Institute. When two people or a group have empathy, understanding, and common goals or objectives, they start to resonate—hearts literally come into coherence.

It starts with balancing our centers of intelligence—mind, heart and body. When we are in alignment, others can sync with us, especially when rallying together for a common cause or passion. This is when mountains can be moved, and great breakthroughs happen. Trust, loyalty, reciprocity, interdependence can all happen with this deep level of social connection. Now, that's some powerful energy!

Action Step:

- Imagine yourself in the shoes of the next person you talk to.

- What might they be feeling?

- What does their body language tell you?

- What might they be looking for from you?

- How will you respond differently now that you have this insight?

The Head Center
of Intelligence

With the different functions of the mind, and the various filters that color our sensory perception, it is difficult to form a truly objective view of the world, and why there are as many views of the world as there are people perceiving it. The more self-discovery and inquiry we pursue, and discipline we practice to quiet our minds, the greater the clarity we gain to be able to discern and live from the purity of our own great-heart.

Objective reality is perceived when the only activity in the mind is observation of what is here, right now. There is no judgment, manipulation, strategizing, planning, or resenting, or comparison to the past or others. The problem is, the mind is prewired to protect the ego through habitual patterns of thought called fixations. Fixations maintain the status quo. There are also defensive mechanisms that trigger automatically when the fixation is challenged. This pretty much encapsulates the personality, and its distorted view of reality. As we've discussed, the only way out of this fiction is to embark on a journey inside, armed with the magnifying glass of self-awareness. This means practicing mindfulness in every moment, catching ourselves in the act. It is difficult to watch the constant train of thoughts, but with knowledge of the particular patterns that dominate the thoughts, it becomes easier to see when you run off the tracks.

Transforming Fixations:
The Higher Beliefs

*H*ave you noticed a pattern with your reoccurring thoughts? You are not alone. We all have habitual ways of thinking that can take us out of the present moment and hamper objectivity. According to the Enneagram, if you are dominant body center, your issues tend to be around autonomy and control, so your thinking gets stuck in one of three fixations: vengeance, laziness, which means forgetfulness about your priorities, or resentment. This happens when feeling out of control, or pressured by someone else's perceived control, or judging that a situation is not being handled properly.

If you are a mental or head type, your issues are around safety and security, and concerns can manifest in three ways: if you feel threatened by what others may want, or time demanded of you, the fixation of stinginess arises out of a need to preserve space and energy. If there is a fear of others hidden intentions, the fixation is cowardice. If there is a fear of pain or discomfort, the fixation is planning pleasant options.

Those who depend primarily on the heart center are concerned most with connection and creating an image that will insure getting and maintaining connection and receiving love and approval. If that is threatened, there are three patterns of thought that take over, depending on your particular type: flattery, vanity, or melancholy.

The first step is awareness of our fixation. The next step is to catch it as the thoughts begin to form, and name it. Call it out. This is future planning, or this is stinginess. Then, look a layer deeper. Ask: What am I feeling threatened by? It may or may not be obvious, but keep up the inquiry. The inquiry itself interrupts the fixation, and if you stay with it, allows a higher belief or virtue to arise.

Just as there are three fixations for each center of intelligence, there are three virtues of higher beliefs that transform the fixated state of mind. For the body center types, the higher belief of truth replaces the pattern of vengeance. The virtue of love replaces laziness, the virtue of perfection, seeing the inherent perfection in everything and everyone replaces resentment.

In the mental dominated types, omniscience or inner knowing transforms stinginess, faith transforms the limiting belief of cowardice, and the higher belief of Work, the ability to focus and complete the work at hand, slows the tendency to obsessive future planning.

For the image types dominated by the heart center, the higher belief in will and freedom transforms the fixation of flattery. Vanity is transformed by hope, the belief that you are valuable just as you are. The habit of focus on what is missing is transformed by knowing that we all come from the same origin which connects us all.

The head or mental center of intelligence is where we search for meaning in the world. Many people end up taking on the worldview of the family and community where they are raised, not questioning it's validity or resonance within themselves. There is often pressure or threats of being ostracized should one question the status quo too far. Religion is one area where adherence to tradition is highly valued from one generation to the next. Unfortunately, there are also harmful, stifling beliefs such as prejudice that are passed on, until someone takes the risk of being an outcast and questions the validity for themselves. This takes courage, one of the virtues that replaces the mental pattern of cowardice.

I blessed that I had parents open enough to allow me to question everything. They knew this was an important step in learning critical thinking. When I was a preteen in junior high school, my parents sent me to confirmation class after school at the Lutheran Church our family attended every Sunday. I remember sitting on the grass out front, waiting to be picked up after class. I was mulling over what we'd been taught, and thought to myself, "why are the Indians (Native Americans) wrong in what they believe? How can you create something out of nothing?" This was my first real experience with questioning, and not taking things I heard at face value, but digging deeper for my own sense of truth. It started me on a spiritual quest that brings me closer to experiencing the Truth within myself every day.

Because there were no teachings I had been exposed to or the maturity to put words to my deep inquiries, my questions went unanswered, and I began calling myself an atheist. My parents allowed my rebellion and didn't require me to confirm a belief I didn't hold. They just asked me to be open to learning. That was my first powerful experience of standing in my truth, and I'm forever grateful that my parents honored it, and let me find my own path to God, no matter how long it took.

This poem explores my journey of spiritual searching, doubt, disillusionment, and coming home to that which spoke to my soul.

Pleasures of Doubt

From the Oxford English Dictionary on the usage of Nothing:
The whole would be like multiplying nothing by nothing the result
would still be nothing.

Stretching out on the lawn in front of the church,
seeds of doubt sprouted inside of me. I don't know
what it was that Pastor Christiansen said
that veered me toward the Red Road.
Sitting there after confirmation class,
two questions formed in my mind:
Why were the Native American Indians wrong in what
they believed, and, How do you imagine nothing?
This is how I debunked the creation story that day.
Though I continued attending confirmation class,

I had entered the vast emptiness of atheism.
A proclamation
hung on my bedroom wall, NO GOD in bright
blue paint.
Small yellow daisies's completed the plaque
made by a friend;
who then decided she would rather wear a cross
around her neck.
I did not graduate and confirm their beliefs.

The blood and bone of Christ
never touched my lips, atoning for my sins.
From those first seeds of doubt

I defied generations, stretching back to the
rocky isle of Tofterey,
lying boldly on the North Sea. From where
Monsina Molina Larsdader Toft
agreed to sail for America in her sister's place,
to join her husband to be.
Outside the Hovde farm, in the Gausdal Valley
near Lillehammer,
ancestors from my other side must have turned over in
their churchyard graves.
I don't know how my geography got so scrambled,
but the explanation
I was reaching for was received by sages in Kashmir,
a few thousand years before.

Such a long way from Norwegian fjords,
or my grandparent's church on Montezuma Avenue.
The red hymnal weighed heavy in my hands.
Wordy lines crammed into verse,
the organ and my voice would never merge.
My heart sings across another ocean,
a haunting raga calling to me,
moved by tamboura and drums.

Making Peace with Fear

Being a head center, or mental type, fear has been with me all my life. Much of the time, I was unaware of it, and ran straight on into challenges. I remember one experience in my tearoom modeling days. In the hotel boutique I modeled for, the manager was in her early twenties, a few years older than me. Her much older boyfriend would come in and yell at her abusively. One afternoon, I'd had enough. He stood just inside the glass doorway, yelling and grabbing her. I got in the middle, right in his face, and told him to stop and to leave right now! I wouldn't let up until he left. I thought he was going to punch me, he was so angry, but I stood my ground.

The fear that can paralyze me is more insidious and comes in the form of doubting myself and fear of losing my freedom, and my financial well being. It is an underlying mental pattern that I flew straight in the face of, always being self-employed, and never knowing for sure when or if the escrow would close, or another client would come. Despite my fears, I have always been persistent and had the tenacity to keep going no matter how long it takes.

In recent years, after divorce, leaving my career and community and starting over, I've become familiar with insecurities about who I am. Everything I identified myself with was gone. Thankfully, I had financial security from the previous real estate boom, but I felt shattered into a thousand tiny shards. My heart was broken. I went through coaches training. During one session, the trainer, David Darst, asked for a volunteer for a demonstration. He said that it had to be someone that hadn't been up before, and whoever got to the chair first was it. I ran up, and just missed sitting in the lap of the woman who beat me there. I went back to my seat, and something in me wouldn't let go—"She's already had a turn!"—I blurted, like a child who didn't get her way. Something in me wanted to be up there. I was right, and she relinquished the chair. I didn't get to sit down. Instead, David sent me to stand facing the full circle of coaches.

He went to the back of the room. "Why do you want to be a coach?"

"I'm passionate about it and I want to help people," I replied, rather lamely.

"That's not good enough. We all want to help people!" He grilled me ferociously, and I stammered until tears rolled down my face. My peers sat there frozen, watching me, and my deep embarrassment in this public display of humiliation. I wasn't angry. I didn't feel like a victim. I knew he was reaching for my depths of strength. He said, "Come here." and I walked to the back of the silent room. "We'll be right back."

He led me out the back door, through the hallway and into the ladies bathroom! He placed me in front of the mirror, red, teary, runny nose face, "Look at yourself." Being the last thing I wanted to do, I looked into the teary eyes. "Your heart can be broken a thousand times and you are strong enough to pull through. Do you know this about yourself?"

"Yes." I stammered. I will never forget those words, and the fierce and loving coaching I received to call forth the best of me. Remembering that confidence he brought out in me, I have withstood many more heartbreaks, and it calls me forth to bring out the best in those I coach.

Cultivating Presence: Mind the Centers

"Before enlightenment, chop wood, carry water.
After enlightenment, chop wood, carry water."
~ZEN PROVERB

When one center has taken over and is running the show, we have a distorted filter that is processing information. We only receive a portion of the story, as told through the motivations and focus of that center. That in turn, pushes the buttons of another center, and the perceptions from that center get out of whack. Don Riso and Russ Hudson, in *Understanding the Enneagram,* said

> ...The scrambling of Centers is the basis of personality. We are not identified with the proper functions of the centers, but with the side effects of their misuse. If our centers were to return to their proper function, our personality, as we know it, would cease to exist. We would still have a personality, but it would be quite different from our habitual experience of ourselves.

Where are your hands? Are your hands receptive and listening quietly in your lap? Are they chopping vegetables, or typing on the keyboard? Are they tying a shoe or drawing a tree, perhaps watering the flowers.

Where are your feet? Are they strolling, taking in the view or running to the next destination? Are they firmly grounded in the earth or floating just above the surface? Are they going one way and your mind going another?

Are you aware of your body? What are the sensations that are happening now? Are you cold, warm, comfortable or cooking? What does the fabric of your clothes feel like against your body? Soft, itchy or silky? Do you feel the air kissing your skin?

What are you feeling? Are you calm, peaceful, or agitated? Are you feeling love in your heart or anger and vengefulness in your gut? Breathe into your heart space and belly. What feelings surface? Can you allow whatever you are feeling to be there? Are there tears behind your eyes, or beginning to roll down your face? Is there anxiousness? Just allow whatever is surfacing to be there, without judging.

If you are reactive, slow down the reaction time with a pause. Ask yourself what the story is that triggered the reaction? Then, what is the core belief beneath the storyline? It may be something like, "I'm not good enough," or "People can't be trusted," "Everyone only thinks of themselves," or "I'm not smart enough or pretty enough", on and on.

If you have a difficult time accessing feelings, take a moment to connect with your heart space. Place your hands gently over your heart and just breathe, quietly. Feel your chest soften and contemplate: What am I missing? What is my heart longing for? What is it that I'm most grateful for? What brings me joy?

Where are your thoughts? Are they with your hands? Are your thoughts where your feet are? What does your mind think? Are your thoughts of the past, future, or present? Is your mind racing from one thought to another, or stuck on one series that keeps repeating over and over? Can you just observe them with no opinion, or trying to change or stop them?

Action Step

Go to my site smarieyoung.com to download the complimentary audio recording:

ACTIVATE YOUR POWER CENTERS
Experience immediate results with this twelve–minute centering practice that will align your power centers for increased grounding, confidence, and ease.

A Shift in Perception

I had a vivid dream several years back. I was in a big house with many people, including my former husband Jim. I was wondering how he'd kept the house all these years. Then, I remembered he was dead. There were brightly costumed women, one with pink, curly hair. I noticed a wall where people had hand painted notes. I went to sleep on a sofa bed in the middle of the room. When I awoke, there was a man getting ready to give a seminar who had written information all over the wall. I apologized for sleeping late and went to find my suitcase to leave. I wondered if the woman who owned the house rented it out for events. I went into a bedroom, where a female security guard frisked me. The curtains flapped open, and I saw outside the window was an atrium with a bed and beautiful plants and flowers.

My life has always been rich with variety and color. The house is me and all the characters in the dream are aspects of me, including my husband Jim. He was a major influence in the way I perceived the world, and still after all these years occupies a place in my mind. I see the dream as a message that I have been asleep to my perceptions and I'm waking up to old ways of seeing and acting in the world that no longer serve me.

Being in commercial real estate for years, the rule of that culture was to always look successful, no matter what. I perceived the consequences of breaking this rule as catastrophic—to lose confidence, get no clients, and have no earnings. This rule became entrenched in me early on, and it affected the way I dressed, where I lived, what I drove, and my politics. It put me in debt and had me living on the edge. During the big recession in the early nineties, I began a quest of personal and spiritual development. My perceptions and that rule were killing my body and my soul. I began a paradigm shift that created a more authentic life and healthier definition of success, which eventually led me to leaving real estate sales and starting coaching.

As a student of meditation, I learned that everything is the manifestation of the Absolute, or God, including me, and you. There is nowhere that energy force is not. I have real glimpses of this, and through meditation, slowly, as my perception shifts and widens, this can become a living experience that I embody all the time. As a manifestation of the great heart, we are constantly performing the act of creation through our thoughts. They create our perception, and, therefore, our world. If we want a different world, it is up to us to create new thought patterns into a different world view.

The great heart is the area of our chest all the way up through the crown of our head, and beyond. Though our thoughts originate in the mind, the great heart has significant influence over the quality of our thoughts. In his book, *The Splendor of Recognition*, Swami Shantananda elucidates for the student a key text of Kashmir Shaivism on the ancient science of the soul called *Pratyabhijna-hrdayam* ("The Heart of Recognition") written by the sage Kshemaraja in the eleventh century. The text outlines three aspects of the mind: the intellect, the ego, and the thinking faculty. The intellect receives sensory information and stores memory; the thinking faculty makes sense of it, categorizes it, and puts words to it; and, the ego relates to it and personalizes it. In this way, we receive information and stimuli from the outer world and signals from within ourselves, through our sensory perception, and the mind discerns, judges, and possesses it with an I, as in I like, I dislike, I feel pleasure or pain.

The goal in meditation is to drop all identification other than as being one with the Absolute. Part of this process is to become the witness of all thoughts and actions without letting the ego appropriate them as its own. When we do this, we naturally drop into the great heart, the home of Universal Energy residing within us. Through meditation, the heart opens, and I can perceive that the essential nature of everything is divine love. To embody this state of love, I just need to connect with my heart.

Paradigm Shift

No longer the particle, but the wave.
Circling, circling, circling the core;
radiating out from the scintillating Blue Light.

Solid is enveloped by ripples of space.
Circling, circling, circling,
intricate patterns gently form, then disappear.

Soft undulations spiral into blackness.
Boundaries become permeable, waves lap,
absorbed into the next, into the next.
Particles merging with waves.
Meditation swallowing illusion.

Integration and Fulfillment

When you have been rigorous with self-inquiry and have been honest with yourself about what you found and committed to change what was no longer working, then you come to know what you stand for. You practice and become proficient at standing in your truth, communicating it clearly, and acting in integrity. You honor yourself and others by holding steadfast to your values.

The more we get to know ourselves, come to peace with our past, and are able to be present in the moment, the more familiar we become with peace and contentment. When we know what is in the deepest part of our heart, both the pain and desire, what we believe, and what is most important, that is when we have a chance for inner fulfillment. We can't stand in our truth, and relay it effectively if we are confused as to what is true for us. When we come face to face with our inner demons—those painful memories, untruths we absorbed, and sabotaging beliefs and self-talk, and root them out by shedding the bright light of self-awareness on them, and being vigilant to catch them and deal with them as they appear, we then give our heart a chance to be heard, and to lead. Most of us lead with fear rather than love, and keep ourselves bound tight by restraints—in self-imposed knots as well as those tied by others.

Rebel Girl

I don't want to lead.
I don't want to follow.
Just leave me alone to live my life.
I am a rebel girl.

I may look like a conformist.
I have a tailored style.
Looks are deceiving.
I am a rebel girl.

I don't think like the girl next door.
Independence is what I crave.
Determination to call the shots;
Overcoming all that's in my way.
I am a rebel girl.

Just watch me now.
I come from behind.
Comfortable in my tailored style;
Quiet is my way.

You live your life,
And I'll live mine.
I am a rebel girl.

Action Step:

Keep asking these questions,
and see if your answers change with time.

- What is most important to me?
  How do I want to live my life?
  If I could do anything, with no restraints,
  what would it be?

- What values do I hold dear?

- What would bring me the greatest happiness?

- What are my most cherished beliefs?

- What do I want/need to take a stand for?

- What kind of person do I want to be?

- What is the legacy I want to leave?

PART TWO

Coming Home: Discovering Essence

Home

Let me turn within
to find accolades.
Give it all up, the wanting
costs too much. The pursued is like
glass and mirrors, cold to the touch
and always beyond reach.
Let me just sit here, now,

warming to my own space
and tend to that spark,
illuminating the unknown.
Then, step on out,
following wherever it goes.
It just might be
the pathway Home.

Trusting Oneself

"I only went out for a walk and finally concluded to stay out till sundown, for going out, I found, was really going in."
— John Muir

When I first attended Al-Anon, a program for families and friends of alcoholics, and was introduced to the twelve steps of Alcoholics Anonymous, I had no concept of a power greater than myself that I was supposed to turn my life over to. My sponsor, Cathy, told me to think of something bigger and more powerful than myself and start there.

I was living in the Coachella Valley, in the southern California desert. The desert is relatively flat, with undulating sand dunes. Rising in steep ascent creating the western border, is the towering Mount San Jacinto. According to Wikipedia, on its north face, it climbs rapidly from Snow Creek over 10,000 feet in seven miles, one of the elevation largest gains in a short distance in the continental United States.

Its peak is snow capped most of the year, and there is a purple hue against stark blue sky. Because of the dryness, there is an intensity to the light. There is not much to filter the brightness and heat of the sun.

Wherever I went around the Valley, San Jacinto was always there, looming in the distance. It was the compass pointing west.

There's a solidity to its massive presence, a sense of timelessness, and permanence. In those days, I loved to bicycle for hours at a time. I lived in Cathedral City then, one of nine valley cities. I'd pedal my way along lush golf courses that laid their green carpet starkly against the white sand, toward Palm Springs, at the foot of San Jacinto. I was taken by the beauty of the landscape in this harsh environment, the acacia, mesquite, palo verde, desert willow trees and many varieties of palms, swaying in the breeze. I felt free as I traveled, propelled by my own strength. Reaching the base of the hills hugging the mountain, the city of Palm Springs grew here, against the shade and wind protection of the San Jacinto Mountain Range.

On a late afternoon ride, I took off on a dirt path, alongside the road. I found a boulder, parked my bike and climbed on top to sit and imbibe the view. An alluvial fan spread out in front of me, crisscrossed by washes cut by from snow melt from mountains above. All led to Eagle Canyon. Sitting there, I felt the mothering energy of the canyon, and the masculine energy of San Jacinto, now obscured by the hills in front of me. These natural parental figures became my refuge, the beginnings of a meditation practice. I'd bicycle here whenever I could, perch on the rock and close my eyes, unburdening myself in prayer and, releasing whatever was troubling me at the time.

After several months of this, one day I got an urge to explore. I got back on my mountain bike and followed a wide dirt trail along the arroyo and came to a spot where it crossed the wash. There was an even larger boulder next to it, and I laid down my bike and crawled on top. Closing my eyes again, I felt the stillness of the desert all around me. Suddenly, the was a loud whirring sound and I jumped and my eyes shot open with a start. A tiny hummingbird was hovering right in front of me, it's iridescent green body glittering behind his long, pointed beak. It was off as fast as it came, but time suspended for a few precious moments, as I felt welcomed to his home.

It was fall, and everywhere I looked, I was surrounded by what appeared to be death. The sweltering summer had relentlessly burned the landscape to skeleton and bone. There wasn't a flower or patch of green anywhere to be seen. As I sat in this dead zone, I was comforted by the cycles of life, death, life. My father had died a few months back and here, for some reason, I felt close to him, amid dried cactus carcasses strewn amongst stick bushes. I dreamed I found a coffin out there.

Another morning, I awoke to a dream of a boulder filling up my kitchen, so I couldn't get in. The kitchen is thought to symbolize your creative energy, and mine was clearly blocked. I had to have the boulder blasted out. A few days later, pedaling down Palm Canyon Drive to my spot, there was a construction crew in the wash. I came to the place my rock was supposed to be, and it was gone. They had blasted it into chunks to use to shore up the banks with rocks! At first I was angry and dismayed, but then I remembered my dream. I had traveled deeper, and there was no going back.

Soon, I wanted my feet on the earth, without tires or asphalt separating me from dirt underneath. I started driving to the canyon and taking off on foot, traversing the Lykken Trail, up the ridgeline overlooking Palm Springs, and Tahquitz Canyon on the backside. Two friends and I took a sunrise hike on Easter Sunday. We stopped briefly at my rock next to the wash, and then headed across to the other side, where the trail picked up again. We crossed different branches of the arroyo, making our way to the mouth of the canyon. There were desert gold poppies, evening primrose, and creosote, yellow daisies, and tiny bluebells. The barrel cacti were flowering, and grasses shimmered in the early light. We came upon a long, flat rock, waist high and big enough for all three of us to sit and stretch out, with the morning sun warming our backs, as we watched the hillsides turn shades of pink, then light up brightly. We offered our gratitude on this day of rebirth to honor the rites of spring. Life, death, life—we are blessed with a new day. We christened our place Meditation Rock, and it became a morning ritual for me.

I explored all over that canyon, visiting two or three times a week for awhile. Whatever I was feeling, it would emerge and release once I entered the mother's loving embrace of the canyon. One day, I was too agitated to sit on Meditation Rock. I took off a new way, letting the trail take me where it may. I stomped as I went, throwing curses to the wind. I was led to a ravine, too steep to enter. Instead, I stood up top, hurling rocks and expletives as far as I could. I was dealing with a client who I'd trusted and after working hard on a transaction for eight months, I didn't get paid. A loophole was found to avoid paying my large commission, and it was to be my only paycheck that year, a struggle to keep afloat in the final throes of recession. Another tough lesson about working for someone I knew couldn't be trusted, thinking I could hold my own. Wounded instincts led me to not protect myself in the proper legal way.

Through the suffering we endure as part of being alive, nature is steadfast. If we submit, naked of all pretence, she cleanses the mud and muck we insist on swimming in. She offers solace in the form of a wider perspective. The larger scheme cannot be avoided when confronted with the vastness and wonderment of her creation. When you walk on earth surrounded by formations carved over eons, the day day-to-day drama suddenly appears insignificant, grounded in the geological sands of time.

Coming home to what?
you might ask.

What else is there beyond my sense perception?

Who am I, really?

Where did I come from and why am I here?

What happens to me after I die?

These are the ponderings of Essence calling us home, into the mystery. Beckoning us to drop the veil and peek under the curtains. They come to us in the quiet hours before dawn when our makeup is off, guard is down, and the smell of brewing coffee hasn't yet hit. That time betwixt and between the dream and waking worlds. If we languor here a little while, then rise quietly, stealth by the sleeping cat, to alight in a cozy corner, journal in hand, we may net some answers, to be held reverently, without grasp. Then it is wise to slip out and soak up the last vestiges of darkness, dew on the grass, quiet streets. Find a hill and face east, at the dawn of a new day.

It is in the stillness of mind and body that Essence is revealed. Slowing down to gaze out at the horizon, stopping to lie down on a large a rock, absorbing its heat, and walking or sitting in meditation. Non-action does not mean inaction. It is the stillness of what is necessary, nothing extemporaneous, that I'm speaking. It is in listening and following the prompting within, from that deep well of integrity that is the revelation of our true nature.

Healing: Remembering the Pathway

*E*ssence is underneath whatever it is that we use to distract ourselves from the pain of living—shopping, drugs, alcohol, food, caffeine, work, working out, books, television, internet, social media, pornography, sex, infatuation, studying, religion . . . and the list goes on. It is not these things in themselves that obscure essence, it's the way we misuse them that they become harmful. When we abstain from our chosen escape mechanisms, such as unhealthy relationships(mine), we soon encounter the pain from which we are hiding—fear, shame, guilt, unworthiness, loneliness, hurt, anger.

Separation from divinity, from our true nature is to experience emptiness, and that can be excruciating. We try to fill that endless hole in our heart with whatever or whoever will help us forget the pain. In my case, it manifested as a fear of abandonment, that caused me to have and hold onto relationships that were unhealthy. I felt incapable of facing the world alone, and I avoided the pain of emptiness with endless dramas and the chaos of alcoholic men who were not sober. I would finally have enough and break it off, only to jump into another.

Infatuation was another drug of choice. The thrill of attraction and new love is intoxicating! When boredom set in, or the drama became too much to bear, I'd quickly find a replacement, and it would begin again. When I joined Al-Anon, my sponsor challenged me to abstain from dating or entering a new relationship for six months. I thought it was an eternity, but somehow I made it. Some years later I fell madly in love, and the newly sober man ended our short relationship and broke my heart. I remember standing in the shower and a knowing came to me that the real love I wanted was inside me, and that I needed to find it. If I didn't love myself, the man I was with would always reflect that back. I was on my own for two years, discovering myself, including the shadow parts, and learned to love all of me. Then, I met my second husband, and we continued the journey together for a time.

In this poem I express the pain of separation as well as the pain of trying to fill the void with a person.

Longing

"When soul rises into lips, you feel the kiss you've wanted." ~Rumi

Separate, alone, detached, lonely,
wanting desperately a deep, loving kiss.
Words pierce like a pin prick, thick tears ooze slowly down.
No relief, only a knowing,

the longing for the other's kiss is not what it's about.

Separation from Self deadens contact from the inside out.
Old dances carry on, in the same sad misstep.
Perfect rhythm just a beat away.
The sound of eternity seems lifetimes from me.

When we accept whatever feelings that arise, and can stay with the pain and discomfort, ignoring the urge to run, they loosen their grip, and after awhile are not so crushing to bear. Apply tender loving care, self-love and a big dose of patience. Reframe the stories, mine the memories for the choicest gems. Know that every step you took was required to arrive at the exact spot you are standing today—every bit of it!

When we have self-awareness and know that we are complete and whole within, we can relate to others in an authentic way and don't have expectations of others to relieve the feeling of being not enough. We all carry a sense of being separate, and different from our own essence and others. Self-inquiry and going within to connect with our true essence that is the same within everyone, heals that painful illusion.

When I forgot my way to essence, there was a feeling of unworthiness and emptiness that no one could fill. I desperately looked to others to save me. I believed no one would want someone so flawed. In response to this belief, I created an image of what I thought others may want and need so they would value me. Hiding behind an image, resentment grew because I was playing a role that wasn't who I am. All of this was beneath level of consciousness, until I opened the front door and began to look within. The front door leads to an inner door, and that door led to my heart.

Joining Al-Anon opened the door. Stepping off that bicycle to sit for awhile in the shadow of San Jacinto, a power greater than myself, cracked the inner door of my heart. Through that crack, some very painful feelings exploded through my body, but I didn't shut the door! I rode through the hills and valleys, experiencing death and rebirth, and my heart opened wide.

Through my inner travels, I arrived home, to who I really am. When I venture out and forget again, I know the well worn pathway back. The door is always open.

It is the quality of interactions that determine the quality of our life. It is our ability to share who we are authentically that creates a satisfying relationship. Yet, how often do we show up and be who we really are? There is so much posturing and image control that happens as we relate to others, and most of it is an ingrained, unconscious habit. We may act tougher than we really feel, or pretend to be weaker than we are to elicit help or sympathy. In business, creating an image of success can be important when you begin, until you gain confidence to step into success. There are many roles we play, parent, sibling, friend, social, boss, employee. We can get so caught up in a particular role that unless you have the awareness that you are stepping into a role, you can fool yourself into believing that's who you are.

There is a lot of fear about revealing our true nature, even to our self. Most of us harbor a deep-seated fear that who we are isn't good enough. As we portray the image of who we think we should be, it reinforces more the notion that we don't measure up. Interactions between one person's image and another's mask leave a lingering feeling that there is something missing, but you can never quite pinpoint what it is.

People that come into our life tend to be similar in personality to someone else that has had a significant impact on us, either positive or negative. We want to either heal the bad experience or relive the positive, or usually some of each. We also are attracted to people that mirror us in some way, often mirroring the hidden traits we have disowned, or don't believe we possess. Because people either remind us of someone else, or mirror us, we often project feelings, thoughts, or characteristics onto others that they may not really have, or at least not to the extent we project onto them. We are often reacting to who we think someone is, rather than to whom they really are.

The poem *Sexual Healing* is about the early years of my budding sexuality. The memories became quite painful when my step-daughter turned thirteen, and I saw what a little girl she still was. She showed me that the story I always told myself about being grown up enough to make those decisions on my own, without influence of the older boys I was with was a blatant fabrication.

Sexual Healing

Old patterns, stubborn memories; rip me open!
Whose story is it? No matter, I keep living it.
Reminisces of a twelve-year old, maybe thirteen.
Shopping-center-Joe, alluring in long hair and a van.
Willingly entering his lair, hoping for love's thrill.
Dropped me a block from home, amazingly,
innocence intact.

And then there was the pervert on the phone. Hours
of conversations to see what made him tick. A planned
meeting, thankfully thwarted by a friend's mom. That
thrill gone; I stepped it up a notch. Red-haired senior,
weed, and Strawberry Hill. Bedroom black-light, bodies
lit from within. Shivers of pleasure, still waiting for the
marriage bed. His mother in the next room.

Next stop, a happening party place at Robert's garage.
Who needs girlfriends anyway? Boys don't betray. Only
Hobbits stealing the matches! Widowed dad upstairs,
drowning his pain. Let's get this over with and grow up
quick; he was twenty-one, and I just fourteen. Where
to go from here? How about a rock and roll band? My
lover screamed dedications to me, acting like the man
he wanted to be. If wishes were horses, then I'd fly too.
Flying past this high-school freshman year, to freedom
and independence, moving out at eighteen.

To present day, many lifetimes passed.
Mid-life now, cell memories persist.
As my body releases old remnants,
I open fully to my lover's kiss.
Basking in the bliss of a mended heart,
innocence retrieved.
The Lord's protection always there,
even if parents were asleep.

Innocence and Responsibility

*M*any years ago, when my stepdaughter was thirteen, these early years of budding sexuality and experimentation came up, and I grieved my lost innocence. I saw for the first time, looking at Jessica, that I was just a child when it happened. The young man was four years older, a senior in high school, and even though I believed I was grown up enough to take care of myself, I was still a child. I could finally see that his mother in the next room, married to an alcoholic, let me down. By allowing us to be in a closed bedroom, and more so, assuming we were having intercourse, she gave me permission to become sexually active. And my parents contributed, too, by not asking questions about where I was or who I was with. A few years later, when I did lose my virginity, it was with a twenty-one-year-old man, and I still believed I was in control. There is a reason for the statutory rape law.

From what I've read, it is common in cases of physical, emotional, or sexual abuse for the victim to take responsibility for what happened to them. It gives a sense of control, but it also sets up a lifetime of shame and guilt. It is not just an inside job. The perpetrator blames the victim, and often so do parents and authorities. We see it played out on the news, in examples such as the rampant rape on college campuses. It used to be a common allowable defense in court to bring up a woman's past sexual behavior or seductive way of dressing as the reason for what happened.

The way out of victimhood is paradoxically, to release the sense of responsibility, and place it where it belongs—on the perpetrator. Only when you absolve yourself of blame, and see the situation realistically, can you be released from the role of victim, and gain true power over the circumstances in your past and present. You cannot change what happened, but absolving yourself of responsibility gives you peace of mind and a clear conscience. It allows what happened to remain in the past, rather than continually repeating scenarios of victimhood to try and resolve and heal what happened. One of the results is that we become able to assume responsibility for our own care and life, which is difficult when holding on to an identity of victimhood. The journey from victim to survivor, and ultimately becoming a whole thriver is a winding, bumpy road, but the reward is great and well worth the effort. This road is best traveled with the help of a compassionate, experienced therapist, mentor, shamanic healer, body worker, or a professional in whatever modality you are most comfortable with. You don't have to do it alone, and usually it takes a team. You may find different healers or modalities more helpful than others depending on the phase of healing you are in. Listen to your intuition, and follow its promptings. I found that I would meet someone or hear about something at just the right time.

The Witness

Be quiet, be silent, and be still. Take time to be with you, with whatever is in front of you. Who is the One looking out of my eyes? Listening to these sounds? Who is the One that remembers my dreams? Who is the One who knows what I am thinking and feeling? Can you hear the answer? Get to know the Knower. Hold it close. Listen intently. This is the Witness; this is Home. Feel where Home resides in your body. What feelings arise? Where? The One that is beyond space and time is also as close as our breath. It is the substance that is essential to everything, animate and inanimate, and it is tender, and soft like black velvet. It is Love, in its purest form. It does not pick and choose, it emanates from everyone and everything equally.

Even when it is fierce and destructive, it still carries the quality of Love. It encompasses all that ever was and all that will be. It is omniscient. The more we live free of escape mechanisms, the greater the contact with our essential nature is possible. How do we know when we are expressing our true nature? We embody and express the virtues in every thought and action. The virtues are essential qualities.

The poem Essence is an attempt to describe the indescribable. Nature provides our closet metaphor.

Essence

Below the chatter
appearance, image, status disappear.

Elusive green flash
sun dipping under blue horizon
red, yellow and pink
paint the sky wisps then
broad strokes

within color, texture, fragrance
where senses cease
lame in the face

of what is unknowable,
yet felt right inside.

Living in Essence

When we contact the deepest part of us, it is like switching on a light in the basement. All the junk we have stored for a lifetime peaks through from the cobwebs. Boxes are stacked on top of one another, ceiling high, layers deep. The oldest and messiest boxes are way in the back in the bottom of the pile. We see they are holding up all the other boxes. If we disturb those, everything will come tumbling down! Maybe that's a good thing, even though spring cleaning isn't on the top of most people's lists. The stale energy of all this junk permeates the whole house and weights it down, zapping its vitality, and resiliency to weather new storms.

Just look at the weight of all that we carry around, stored in the deep recesses. We don't realize what a life-drain it is. All that junk seeps in and dulls the magnificence of the essential qualities. The jewel tones that naturally shimmer with light become dull and listless with a thick film of dust. Baba Muktananda, a great meditation master who is very dear to me, said, "Take a broom and sweep your heart."

John O'Donohue, in his book, *Anam Cara: A Book of Celtic Wisdom* said,

> There is a healing for each of our wounds, but this healing
> is waiting in the indirect, oblique, and nonanalytic side

of our nature. We need to be mindful of where we are damaged, then invite our deeper soul in its night-world to heal this wounded tissue, renew us, and bring us back into unity."

One reason many people find it difficult to be still, to meditate is that whatever we are avoiding, eventually surfaces. When we persist and allow whatever arises to just be, without judgment, and just observe whatever feelings and sensations arising, we come to know the Witness, who is infinitely compassionate. When we remove the lid, the carefully crafted facade begins to crack. The grips of our identifications start to loosen, and this is frightening at first. Who are we, really? We no longer know. If we have the courage to continue to close our eyes and follow our breath for longer periods, a much richer, truer version of ourselves emerges. Maybe not as put together as we hoped, but infinitely more fun to be around. The wonderful ability to laugh at oneself and life can be cultivated and welcomed.

Instead of an open-hearted compassion, curiosity and willingness to engage suffering without running away, we find a compulsive need to criticize, and then fix, ourselves and others in order to take away their pain and protect ourselves. We mistake false compassion for real compassion and wonder why we never feel really healed and whole. And so it goes; we dream of relief and fulfillment, but settle for shallow and unsatisfying substitutes for real life.

According to John Davies, in *The Diamond Approach: An Introduction to the Teachings of A.H.Almaas,*

> When we are cut off from our natural strength, our energy and passion are less available. The sense of expansive

vitality escapes us and we feel weak. To make up for this, we push too hard or strain to capture that passion. We try to convince the world and ourselves that we are not as weak as we feel. Bitterness or hostility flavors our activities and relationships. We then mistake this fake strength for the real thing, and we are caught on a merry-go-round of proving ourselves. The harder we try to prove our strength, the more we reinforce our weakness.

Surface satisfactions come and go, fleeting and never reaching to the depths of the origin of our angst. At some point, when the suffering is acute enough, we turn our gaze around and look within. Someone said the longest journey is from the head to the heart. It is because it takes so long to make that U-turn. While it may be the longest journey, it is also the most rewarding, for what we are looking for in the myriad of travels and thrill seeking can only be found within our own heart. A beautiful quote by A.H. Almaas from his book, *Essence With The Elixir Of Enlightenment*:

> Essence is then the teacher, essence is then the taught. Essence is then the freedom. Essence is then the realization. Essence is then the fulfillment. Essence is then the being. Essence is then the very nature and substance of the individual. Essence is then the experience, the experienced and the experience. Essence is then the truth. Essence is then the nature of all reality.

Connection with essence is to connect with our core. That core is the same in everyone and everything, although it shines through us refracting our unique radiance. It is the still point that never changes, and never dies, and is said to be the only thing that is real. Everything else is impermanent, an illusion of our mind, according to Vedanta, a philosophy from India. There is suffering in a world of constant change. There is nothing to hold onto that doesn't shift and move out from under us, and it is very real! It is real, and I believe, all a different face of God, the good, the bad, and the ugly included. Without an anchor wedged into some certainty, we are adrift in fear. Depending only on our self to maneuver through life takes armoring and stubbornness, and we become wary and cynical. We form a necessary shield to protect our little territory, manufacturing certainty and security from whatever outside forces we can find. There is a strong need to control one's environment and an overwhelming sense of sadness for the lost connection with ourselves and others. A sense of malaise underlies everything, and we do our best to cover it up with our choice of escape and survival mechanisms. We use the mechanisms that are most effective over and over until we believe this is who we are. We spend time everywhere, except in our own heart. This is the basis that forms the nine personality types found in the Enneagram.

Underneath the personality of habitual emotional and mental patterns and defense mechanisms, there is a purity of remembering, of longing for deep connection. We search outside ourselves and come up empty time and time again.

Gently but consistently, intelligently and knowingly, Essence puts pressure on us to start longing for it. Then it provides us with the insights, the intuitive knowledge that helps us understand our disharmony. And finally, it shows itself, culminating our experience by manifesting itself as a complete and absolute resolution for our conflicts.

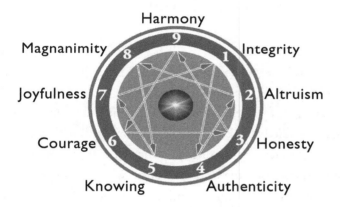

Harmony

Magnanimity

Integrity

Joyfulness

Altruism

Courage

Honesty

Knowing

Authenticity

Self Actualization occurs when we embody the outstanding qualities of all the Enneagram styles.

Walking Toward Home

*P*eace, contentment, and true fulfillment are elusive until we do an about face and take the plunge, diving to the depths of our own being. The empty promises of the barrage of advertisements for bright-shiny-objects and adrenaline filled thrills, constantly thrown in our face in our consumer society, render life meaningless. The real prize is in coming home. Tapping into the Source within through focusing on the breath to quiet the mind, eventually leads us to quit our endless wandering. What is the genuine pot of gold at the end of the rainbow? It's finding comfort being in your own skin, a warm feeling emanating from the heart. At its core, it's all love. It's steadfastness and trust, shaped from love, faith and hope. It is always there and utterly dependable.

Once we learn the path there, and visit regularly, we are gradually relieved of the burdens of lifetimes. A tremendous weight is lifted when we realize we aren't alone, and we don't have to do it by ourselves. There is a benevolence that pervades everything, that will carry it for us, and absorb it all. It can only take what we are willing to give up. Contentment arises not from any outside happening or circumstance, but as a natural state of being conscious and connected. In this state, there is a flow of energy that can be discerned. We can feel it if we swim in the flow of the energy, or paddling hard upstream. Riding the current of the benevolent Source is smooth sailing. When we are blown back against a strong headwind, we know we are headed the wrong direction.

Encountering resistance strengthens our resolve. It takes discrimination to know whether we are pushing ahead for selfish reasons, or for the greater good. Our personal agenda doesn't always jive with the natural flow of what's best—the goodness that is meant for us. When we fight it, there are struggles and dramas. It is often in hindsight that we see the wisdom of the flow, and learn not to resist. Swimming with the current is effortless. When we swim opposite, we eventually get so worn out, if we continue, we go under. Life is a great barometer. It will show us when we get off track. When we are connected to the energetic flow, there is a sense of being carried along, especially through difficult or painful times. We understand that we aren't the one making anything happen. Things line up and fall into place.

It is not so much that everything goes our way. We learn to trust that whatever the outcome, it is for the highest good. Detached from the outcome, we have faith that there is a higher purpose, and everything that happens leads to the ultimate fulfillment of that purpose—our self-actualization. Thy will, not my will!

When we plug into the Source that flows through everything, directly inside our self, our personal power increases manifold. It lights us up, purifies our body, heart, and mind, and gives us the strength and vitality for right action. It gives steadfastness, and the resolve to stay on course inspite of obstacles. This life force is magnetic; it attracts to us whatever deeply held beliefs think we deserve. Our feelings of worthiness or lack thereof determines our success. Whatever we believe about ourselves in the innermost recesses is what we get, no matter how many affirmations we repeat. Our outer circumstances reflect what is going on inside. More accurately, our reaction to outer circumstances is the best indicator of our inner state of being. The definition of happiness is wanting what you have.

Practicing gratitude for what you have is one of the best ways to connect with your heart, the home of Source, our essential nature. Giving heartfelt thanks for everything that happens opens the channel wide for that infinite energy of divine love to flow. On my last trip to India, I was celebrating Diwali, Indian New Year, in a temple. There was a ritual taking place, in honor of Lakshmi, the goddess of abundance. As I watched the offering of precious oils, spices, milk, coconut, and ghee accompanied by ancient Vedic mantras, I offered my gratitude, and thought of what I should ask of abundance on this auspicious night. It came to me that all I needed to ask for was to be in the constant state of bliss I was experiencing in that moment. No matter what side the pair of opposites is playing, happy or sad, pain or pleasure, gain or loss, my inner state would remain the same. If I had that, then whatever happened on the outside, I would remain in equanimity, experiencing the love that is me.

There are a thousand paths that lead to the inherent joy that is our birthright. It is up to us to choose one and start walking.

Walking Toward Home

Inner Nature beckons
Resist no more
Follow the longing
Answer the tug. Begin.

Breathe in long
follow it in
stay awhile
warming your hands
in the fire of Love.

The thirteenth century mystic poet, Rumi said,

Out beyond ideas of wrongdoing and rightdoing, there is a field.
I'll meet you there.
When the soul lies down in that grass, the world is too full to
talk about. Ideas, language, even the phrase 'each other' doesn't
make any sense.

The following poems come from the countless hikes into Eagle Canyon, my refuge in the Coachella Valley. In the blistering heat or the crisp chill of winter, I'd return again and again and let myself be taken on whatever path called to me. Invariably, I'd finish with a feeling of gratitude for the release of my troubles and a renewed enthusiasm for life.

Protector of the Maidens, inspired by the poem, *Keeper of the Fire and the legends of the Cahuilla Indians about Tahquitz*

Protector of the Maidens

Long ago there lived a chief who lived in a great canyon, sheltered from the blowing sand of the desert. He had all he needed; a tall waterfall, fed from mount San Jacinto above, groves of palms and abundant soil to grow maize and beans.

But after awhile, the great chief grew restless. There were no rivals to fight, and the children were too loud.

There were two young maidens he particularly disliked. They had eyes for his son and not him.

Each time they grew near, vying for his son's affections, he grew angrier.

Finally one day, his rage could no longer be contained. The earth began to violently shake as he grabbed them and ran.

Suddenly, from the top of the waterfall came a thunderous roar, as Chief Tahquitz threw the maidens over the edge.

They landed on the rocks far below, bones scattering on both sides of the shallow creek.

The earth continued its tumultuous quivering, until deep fissures separated the desert floor.

When all was quiet again, Earth Mother came and gathered the bones and torn flesh of each of the maidens, for she would not allow her daughters to come to such a fate.

She tightly wrapped them both in fresh palm
fronds, and carried them to the canyon next door,
separated from Chief Tahquitz by towering cliffs.

Initiation

I took her to Meditation Rock,
leaving her there to be guided
through a few rotations of the earth.
This rebel within, my only child;
she needs more than me as her mother,
to show her, teach her the lessons

she missed. Those tough lessons
that can be like a hard hit by a rock.
I left her there, under tutelage of the Great Mother,
to have the grand master as her guide.
A great opportunity for this child
to ground herself with the earth.

A suburban girl rarely touches the earth.
She misses the gifts of nature a rural child
receives, like how to warm herself lying on a rock,
the honing of her instincts to be a good guide.
Constantly tuned to the frequency of Earth Mother,

listening for the whisper of wisdom from Mother,
as in Great Mother Earth.
A true guide, sometimes gentle, other times harsh,
the lessons she imparts

are solid as rock, and light as air.
Stay here and align my dear,
dance with the heart of a wild child.
Move in nature, walk with her,
climb up and dance atop that rock.
Re-establish your relationship with earth.
She teaches you to let go, trust your own center,
where she talks to you.

This is a rite of passage my child,
An initiation to the lessons given in love,
by the creator and destroyer.
She is sunrise, stream, wind and sand.

My child, have you learned your lessons,
experienced the transformative fire of Mother Earth?
She is your inner guide, a flame simmering like molten rock.

Silence

*I*f we practice becoming silent, and listen to our habitual thought patterns and emotions as they surface, we can begin to have mastery over what comes out of our mouth. When anger or fear arises, we can pause, step back and make a conscious decision how we want to handle the situation. When we catch our self with negative thoughts about another person, we can ask our self, "Is this really true", or am I projecting an old, false belief onto them, or something that was true in our past, but is no longer the case in this time, place, and with this person.

In *A Path with Heart*, by Jack Kornfield, he says,

> Repeated thoughts or stories are almost always fueled by unacknowledged emotion or feeling underneath. These unsensed feelings are part of what brings the thought back time and time again. Future planning is usually fueled by anxiety. Remembering of the past is often fueled by regret, or guilt, or grief. Many fantasies arise as a response to pain or emptiness. The task in meditation is to drop below the level of the repeated recorded message, to sense and feel the energy that brings it up. When we can do this, then the thought will no longer need to arise, and the pattern will naturally fade away.

Twice I've had the amazing experience of five days of silence during an ashram retreat. Silence does not mean just not talking—that's the easy part. It also means silencing the chatter of the mind, which seems next to impossible! When the conversations stopped, and my mind couldn't grab on to what others were saying or I was going to say next, all of a sudden I was listening to my inner thoughts, and could get a grasp on how busy my mind really is. It is a non-stop commentary of opinions, judgments, desires, and aversions. It's a wonder how I ever create anything through the din of that noise! Each day my mind became less filled with thoughts. Space opened within, and a feeling of peacefulness descended upon me. By the fifth day, there was a part of me that didn't want to leave that quiet sanctuary of silence. It is a place I yearn for, and always know I can go back there. It's as close as my heart.

This poem expresses the longing for the physical presence of the spiritual teacher. It is a critical phase of the spiritual journey of turning within for guidance instead of seeking outside oneself. The longing can be felt as a pain in the heart, and tears release the pain and open the heart. The stillness and silence of meditation allows the pain to surface. Silence opens access to the deep wisdom that we inherently have, for we ourselves are the One we are looking for.

I Cried for You

I cried for you to notice me.
I felt so small and insecure.
I cried for you to notice me.
I ached for your embrace.

I watched you, and I followed you.
I was angry when you wouldn't meet my gaze.
I cried for you to notice me.

I started dreaming of you, but you were so far away.
Each dream you came a little closer.
Once you hugged me while I cried.

I cried for you to notice me.
Then I dreamt I rubbed your feet.
I cried for you to notice me, and
then I turned my gaze inside.
And there you were all along.

All I had to do was look at all the gifts I've received,
To feel your love for me.
My heart opened in love for you.
In loving you, I am loving me.

To remember you is all I need to feel your love inside.
I imagine your form and feel the vast power within.
I owe my life to you; I willingly give it and disappear.
All that's left is endless love.
I cry for you no more.

Messages in Dreams

One day, there was a substitute teacher when I arrived for my fourth grade class. Instead of following the lesson plan, she spent the morning telling us the importance of our dreams. She described the beautiful imagery found in dreams and the symbols that represent a hidden language dreams use to reveal secrets about ourselves. I was enthralled, and I have never forgotten the impact of that day. It opened a new world inside of me, one that I've been in tune with ever since.

Not everyone remembers dreams. There is a delicate stance one must take to retrieve these nightly dramas. It requires a slow waking up process, a time spent in the in-between world of foggy awareness, in the silence of the mind when first waking up, before it revs into full gear. It's like gently pulling a thread with just an image or word from a dream. My invitation to you is to pull it and see the rest of it unfold and come alive again; coaxing it gently, from the dream-sleep world to the world of conscious thought. Once you have it, write it down, along with your impressions. Sometimes, when I write just a piece I held onto, the rest of the dream unfolds on the paper.

I heard the scientist and writer, Gregg Braden say in an interview, that it isn't so important to remember the content of the dream, as much as the feeling you have coming out of it.

That can give clues as to whether you are feeling stressed, or have unresolved anger, or are in a state of love and contentment. Just to lie there with the feelings is enough.

Dreams can be prophetic, revealing a direction to take, or the answer to a question that has our conscious mind stumped. When I go to bed with a confusion or challenge, when I wake up, most of the time, the answer is revealed. It is upon first awakening that we have the most direct access to our inner selves. It is a highly creative time, because we have access to the creative unconscious. I find that intuitions about others are revealed to me in dreams.

A few years ago, I had a dream of Baba Muktananda, a spiritual master who I feel a close affinity with, standing with another spiritual teacher that I had no familiarity with, yet I knew his name. I remembered the dream in vivid detail, which is always a clue that there is an important message. It was right before a trip to India, where I go for spiritual retreat, study, and volunteer work. When I got to India, I researched in the library about the other teacher. I didn't find anything, but days before I was to leave, I was in the library looking at the poetry section, and there was a brochure of a sustainable community in South India called Auroville, which was founded by his disciple and successor, a French woman he called The Mother. It had been misfiled and seemed to be there just for me.

The next year, returning for my annual stay, I met a woman who lived in Auroville. She invited me to visit. It seems clear that the message of the dream was still unfolding. I felt like I was following breadcrumbs to the next clue. Although I never heard back from the woman who invited me, I visited Auroville on my last trip to India in 2011. I didn't have any earthshaking revelations about why I was led there, but I'm glad I went. I've never had a dream that has unfolded so slowly, or that has prompted me to pursue it for so long or far-reaching after it appeared. I am still open to receive whatever the message or the lesson is that the dream has offered.

Journaling is another way to access the deep recesses of mind and heart. I have volumes collected from different stages of my life. Two of my biggest regrets are around my journals. The first, I tore up my journal after my jealous high school boyfriend found it and read entries about a previous boyfriend. The other was turning in my whole journal, rather than the last entries, at the end of a college class, where it was required writing. The instructor never returned it, and when asked, said she had lost it. I regret losing the entries that were snapshots of my thoughts and feelings at those earlier stages of life.

Journaling taps into feelings I'm unaware of, and to the inner wisdom I'm sometimes amazed I have. My entries sometimes take the form of poetry, especially during extended periods of meditation, and when I'm going through an emotional upheaval. The free verse, images and metaphors of poetry are very much like the symbolic language of dreams. The creative impulse of poetry seems to come from the same place. Poetry is a cleansing form of writing that brings to the surface feelings I'm uncomfortable with or unaware of. During a major life transition, writing a daily poem nurtured the healing process and helped me to navigate change—to grieve the past and make space to bring in the new.

Start your own rebellion. I've left the poems in this book raw and uncut. They are an expression of my inner soul. Give your soul child a voice, give your wild self permission to sing, paint, or build sandcastles. Whatever turns you on and lights you up. Just do it!

For many of us, there are layers and layers of sadness and grief that need an outlet, and permission to be seen and felt. Cry me a river is what it feels like sometimes, until that river runs dry. As long as we keep it damned up, it zaps all our vital energy in the effort. It can be such a relief to let it flow and a comfort to know that we won't drown in the process. Although, depending how many losses and years of tears are held up behind that dam, the torrent can be treacherous for awhile. Seeking a compassionate friend, professional therapist, or coach to listen and help you navigate rough waters may be a wise and supportive choice in self-care. I sought the listening ears of all three through difficult periods in my life, and I'm grateful that I did. Now, for the most part, the tears I shed are for present heartbreaks. I think there are always shades of the past that come back bittersweet along with each new loss. We are always learning, healing and releasing the past, which opens space in our heart to reveal the splendor that is held there. When my father died, I read about a poet who said every loss she feels her heart breaking open. My heart physically ached for a long time after and I would often think of her words of wisdom, and welcome the pain.

Arianna Huffington, in *The Fourth Instinct: The Call of the Soul*, talks about the poignancy of times of grief:

> Holding on to the thread of pain, although it may drag us to our knees, is an act of courage—and of trust. We have all heard the clichés about what life is not—a bed of roses, a bowl of cherries, a barrel of laughs. Parents die. Marriages crumble. Children get sick. In these moments, false idols topple. But in the empty places they once stood,

we may, if we will look, find the grace of God. In these places, there are no distractions, no excuses—indeed, there is nowhere left to hide."

The following poems capture loss and reflection. There is an unburdening through words, although the words aren't really adequate to express what is felt. Through unburdening, a deeper connection is forged to the essence within the heart.

Heartache

A lifetime of grief I didn't know I carried.
A love lost, buried too deep to be found.

Unrequited love lay heavy upon my heart,
it longed to unburden the load and break free.
Numbing pain pushed through a path of discovery,
along the way, a deep love of self emerged.

Courage opened the door, faith dug it up,
And God unveiled himself to me.

The Universe is contained within;
only grace can reveal the wealth.
All knowledge is received
through that aching heart.

Being There

Even when my eyes are closed, I know when you are in the room.
These words from my father on his deathbed are etched
forever in my memory. I stayed with
my parents in the days before he died. We had just
learned that he was terminal, and there was no point in
treatment. I was in shock, and needed to stay busy.
I grocery shopped and cleaned the garage. One day, when
I went in to check on him, he said those words as I
turned to go.

They haunted me for years afterward. I wished
I could have just sat there with him. Words were not
needed at that point. Everything had already been said.
He just needed the comfort of my presence. Now I
know, even though I was not able to sit with him long,
he knew that I was there with them taking care of things,
and welcoming guests to say their goodbyes.

There are many ways to convey love that are more
meaningful than words.

PART THREE

LIVING *in* AUTHENTICITY

Looking behind, I am filled with gratitude,
looking forward, I am filled with vision,
looking upwards I am filled with strength,
looking within, I discover peace.

~QUERO APACHE PRAYER

Change Your Name, Change Your Life

Over the last several years, I've gained firsthand knowledge about how powerfully our names shape our identity and affect our own and other's perceptions of us.

When I started writing poetry, I began expressing feelings and truths that I had been afraid to speak out about. Two poems in the first section of this book are about the feelings that came up in tough relationships, that swung between helplessness/ victimhood and righteous anger, and the beginnings of personal power. In the poem, Flowers and Nice, about being passive aggressive, I used a strong expletive. My then husband, Bob suggested I might want to use a pen name, since I was sharing the poems aloud at poetry readings.

In the meditation tradition I practice, it is customary to request and receive a spiritual name. Using a spiritual name can aid in loosening the strong hold our ego has on preserving our identity, which is one goal of meditation. I had never thought about requesting one, but his comment sparked its consideration. Shortly thereafter, I read a story describing a woman asking for a spiritual name and being told she already had one—Mary. My middle name is Marie, so I took that as a message. But, I couldn't imagine myself as Marie.

That summer, my mother-in-law, Clarissa, broke her hip and was put in a nursing home. By early October, no longer able to swallow, she was unable to eat. Her systems were shutting down, and she slipped in and out of consciousness. I wanted to do for her what I could not do for my own father—to sit quietly with her through the last stages of her dying process. I was much younger when my dad died, and it was such a huge loss. I was too vulnerable to just sit quietly with him. I visited Clarissa daily. The day before she died, I came into her room, and sat in the chair beside the bed. I reached for her frail, wrinkled hand and saw she was holding something. Her fingers were grasping the Mary bead of a rosary. The priest must have left it earlier when he gave her last rites. She had hung on for days longer than anticipated with no food or drink. I felt the compassion Mary embodies rise within. I invoked her benevolent grace, "Mary is waiting for you. She will take you in her arms and take care of you."

I left soon after, and my husband and I were awakened just after midnight with the news she had passed. We went to her bedside to say goodbye; the rosary was still clutched in her hand. A few months later, on New Year's Day, I hosted a meditation gathering at our home. Someone brought a guest named, you guessed it—Mary. In a conversation with her later, she asked for my full name. I answered Sally Marie. She said, "Sally doesn't fit you, you should go by S'Marie." Sally never felt right to me either. Something about S'Marie grabbed me, and slowly, the idea grew. I adopted it for a pen name, and asked family and friends to use it. Some loved ones made the transition willingly, and others resisted strongly. Having had a well established name in business, I thought I'd never be able to switch completely to my new name.

Once it took root, the name became stronger than my twenty-five year career identity and the life that surrounded it. When I took a stand and asked everyone in my personal life to use my new name, my whole life crumbled over the next year. In the space of a few months at year end, Bob and I separated, and I took a four-month retreat in India. When I returned, I had no home to go to. Our real estate company was already closed, and my eighteen year-old-cat had died while I was away. I packed and moved to San Diego. Life as I knew it was over.

The name change simply reflected a fundamental change in who I was that had been in process for years. My life no longer fit who I had become. A few years back, someone told me about the old saying, "Change your name, change your life." I asked myself: "Would I have still done it, had I known?" The answer is "yes."

What's in a Name?

Sal Bug, Salamander, Silly Sally. Who is this girl? I can't relate. These silly names that tease and don't fit—it's enough to give a girl a complex! It started with a first grade primer, *Dick, Jane, and Sally*. Little Sally was the baby in the book, and I was big Sis. No kid told me what to do! I was serious Sally, felt all grown up at three. The oldest child of two, I was no one's Little Sally.

Shy Sally indeed, these childish names only embarrassed me. As I got older, the nicknames continued, they just changed: My Gal Sal, Mustang Sally! Sally in the Alley, Mission Valley Sally, and one I kind of liked—Long Tall Sally.

As a thirty-something, I started a meditation
practice, and soon, poetry was coming through. I hadn't
written a poetic word since junior high. When in one
poem, my dark side popped out, a bit of hard profanity
fit the bill. My husband said if I was going to read it
publically, a pen name would be good. I thought, Sally
doesn't fit me anyway, never has. So I laid the intention
to find a spiritual name to use.

The answer started coming soon thereafter,
provided in creative ways. I read a story about a woman
who asked my meditation teacher for a name. She told
her, *"You already have a spiritual name—Mary."*

Not Sanskrit or exotic, but there it was plain as
day. She was named at birth, after Mary, Mother Divine.

I wrote a line in a poem, *"Hail Mary, make your presence known."* Known to whom? I thought.

I then picked up a book off my shelf, bought
long before, titled *Missing Mary*. Reading those pages,
I was fascinated to find there are many names of the
Compassionate One. Not raised Catholic, I never heard
of the Queen of the Universe. Though I had experienced her love a few years before, at the side of a loved
one's dying bed. I saw frail hands clutching a rosary, so I
prayed for the Blessed Mother and she came. With open
arms, she paved the way, for my mother-in-law to travel
the Eternal Highway.

Something stirred deep inside me. An old memory
surfaced. In a store one day, a beautiful bracelet caught
my five-year-old eye. My parents gave in to my pleas, and
I walked out with pride. Resting gently on my wrist, the

shiny blue bracelet reflected the sun. The beauty
of that soft, blue light only revealed the imbedded
form of Our Lady on closer inspection at home.
"You can't keep it, Mary's a mere mother. Luther taught that we
worship only the Lord. No false idolizing allowed. Pleeeese! No!"
I screamed and cried as I walked, bracelet in hand,
knocking at the door, three houses down. Prompted by
my parents, I offered my beloved bracelet to Shea, my
Catholic best friend.

At age thirteen, I declared myself an atheist. Who
needs God, anyway! Inside, an iron curtain descended,

I was powered by my own steam. Years went by,
losses ensued, and life was experienced from the outside
looking in, so it seemed. Then, when edges started to
soften, a spiritual journey began.

Turning back to the book, *Missing Mary*, there I
saw it in black and white. Another name for the divine
Mother: Ava Maria, wait, that's my middle name! Sally
Marie, the birth name given in honor of both my
Grandmothers. How funny, snuck one by old Luther,
didn't She? Marie, Queen of Heaven and Earth.

Marie sounds rather staid; it was my ancient
Grandma for heaven's sake!

It still didn't sink in, what I'd been given at birth,
so a messenger was sent. A friend of mine brought a
wise woman named Mary to my home that New Year's
Day. Before leaving, Mary asked, *"what's your full name?"*
After I answered, she said: *"Do you think the name Sally fits*
you? I don't. Come out of hiding and be who you are! To me,
you are S'Marie."

I finally got it. I was blessed at birth with a spiritual name, a name that invokes the Mother Divine. From that day forward, I will always be, S'Marie.

What is Authenticity, Anyway?

After reflecting on this question, I came up with this simple definition: Authenticity is when your thoughts, feelings, actions, and words all match. But sometimes we have to fake it 'til we make it, so it goes deeper than that. And we all have many roles we play. How is it possible to be authentic in all of them? Is there just one that is *the real me?*

I spent the first half of my life feeling like I was living on the outside looking in. I played the role of good student, and then there was a rebellious underside that I hid in a secret life. Then I played the role of serious businesswoman and young wife, and the rebel girl stayed under wraps, appearing mostly on Friday afternoons at Happy Hour.

When I got into therapy and began spiritual pursuit, my goal was to heal the split and live on the inside looking out. Over the years, I've discovered that although I play many roles, there is an authentic core that always shines through, if I let it. The secret I learned is not to identify with the role, but with the part in me that witnesses the role-playing. There is a teaching, "The Self Is the Actor." All our social interactions are roles, parent, child, business-owner, teacher, spouse, student, friend, sports enthusiast, employee, boss, subordinate, writer, entrepreneur, yogi, bicycler.

Underneath all roles and names there is a core essence that is the same in all of us. The more we identify with our core self, the more it shines through us and connects to that place in everyone else. Then, no matter what role we are asked to play, our heart shines through. We are real, and more joyful as full participants. People who are authentic are naturally charismatic, because they touch a familiar place within us all. There is recognition. We want to be around them, because they reflect the best in us, the gemstone that sparkles brightly when masks are dropped.

It is not easy to enter the authentic life. Sometimes it drags us in, kicking and screaming. We spend so much time trying to find what makes us happy, and fitting into the image we created for a happy, successful life, that we lose ourselves in the mix. We conveniently swept under the carpet pieces of ourselves and our past that didn't jive. We go along with the cultural norms in order to fit in, look good, and not create too many waves. There comes a point when we must break the mold we stuffed ourselves into and run wild and free. We must say what we think and how we feel, and live to our full potential. There is so much talent, passion, and genuine caring that is buried underneath the weight of "shoulds."

When we break open the shell and our authentic selves begin to emerge, we feel the pain of the constricting prison we have pretzeled ourselves into. As we stretch out and our lungs fill with fresh air, we remember and feel the collective consciousness of being held down, smothered, and shut up. Expressing our anger and indignation at the injustices we endured and see in the world is a natural and necessary outpouring. Turning that into appropriate action is the next step in our personal and collective evolution. Yet, we cannot do it alone. Changes do not come about through self will alone. We must tap into our essential nature, which is part of the collective Essence. Andrew Harvey, in *The Hope: A Guide to Sacred Activism* says:

> Only constant spiritual practice can deepen your reali-
> zation of essential unity with the One so that you can
> begin to face, from the strength and joy that realization
> gives you, the darkness you must confront in yourself and
> the dynamics of the world. It is only by realizing One
> Consciousness in its essential aspect of transcendent bliss
> and peace within yourself that you can begin to face the
> ferocity of its alchemical dance of good and evil, light
> and dark, in reality. Unless you face this ferocity without
> fear or illusion or denial, you cannot work effectively for
> change in a time like ours."

When we tap into the inner power of strength and bliss, we begin to speak with our authentic voice. Then we are no longer willing to hold in the righteous anger about the suffering and injustice we see and feel in the world. The inner work we do ripples out and affects the world around us. There are some that are not content to leave it at that. These are the people that become sacred activists. We all can be a sacred activist in our own way, for the cause we are most passionate and care most deeply about.

The world today is crying out to return to balance. Mother Earth is heaving and weeping in great torrents under the weight of imbalance. There is a call from many fronts to embrace the Divine Feminine, and embody her way of being. Not to swing completely the other way, but to balance the patriarchal values and combine the best of both into actualized human beings who care for the planet, the cosmos, and all its inhabitants, both sedentary and non-sedentary. Andrew Harvey, speaks of this union of the masculine and feminine qualities in *The Hope:, A Guide to Sacred Activism:*

> This return of the force of the authentic Divine Feminine conveys to us, for the first time in human history, on a grand scale and with real potential for transformation, what we might call the Wisdom of the Sacred Marriage—a wisdom that fuses all opposites, "masculine" and "feminine," scientific and mystical knowledge, technological and spiritual power—within a vision of a Sacred Activism that can not only help preserve the world, but birth a new Divine Humanity. It is perhaps because of this—because they see this Wisdom-and-Love-In-Action beginning to manifest with great power on the earth—that the forces of domination and exploitation are wreaking havoc everywhere. It is as if they know that their days may be numbered, that a new vision of Divine Force is coming to transfigure the terms and conditions of life on earth, and so they will do anything—even risk the extinction of the earth itself—rather than lose their hold.

What Can I Do?

I slept and dreamt that life was joy. I awoke and saw that life was service.
I acted and behold, service was joy. —Rabindranath Tagore

The sun still rises and sets
offering its radiant colorscape
painted across the sky.

Soft light infuses the room,
a bridge between nightly respite
and new opportunity.

Between the fullness of light
with all its activity, and the stillness of night,
 is twilight.

If I align myself with the sun and the moon
and the tides, there are answers there,
in the transitions.

In between is endless space.
Lose myself in space,
and daylight brings
inspired action.

Being informs doing.

Our Mother is Weeping

Our Mother is weeping. The ice is melting, the ice is melting, Mother is weeping. The warning from the native people in the north letting us know the ice is melting. I sometimes feel helpless in the face of all the destruction. Mother Earth is shaking with the rape and pillage that has been rocked upon her. I read about a Chief from the far North Arctic Circle who came down from the to speak in front of a United Nation summit to warn the people of the world, "The ice is melting in the North, the ice is melting. Stop what you're doing Now. You are destroying our Mother."

It's another example of clouded perception. The naysayers have us believe it's not happening and climate change is not real, that it has nothing to do with our choices, actions or behavior. Oil companies bribe scientists to tell their convoluted version of the story to preserve profitability and keep that black gold flowing. And despite overwhelming evidence to the contrary, many people are still fooled. It is denial caused by fear, actually terror, for we are looking at annihilation, the end of life as we know it. It is too big to grasp. We must have compassion for those who are not willing or able to see and yet we must wake up and change and do what we can to help our Mother.

In 2011, I visited southern India to see an experimental international community with sustainable principles, outside of Pondicherry, called Auroville. I hired a driver and traveled a few hours after staying four days in Ramanashram, an ashram in Tiruvannamalai, Tamil Nadu, where a revered spiritual teacher named Ramana Maharshi had lived. While there, I ate on the floor, with a banana leaf for a plate, and my fingers as utensils. I walked a cobblestone path daily up the sacred hill called Arunachala to meditate in a cave where he had lived much of his adult life. There were peacocks in the gardens and monkeys along the path. Local merchants set up tables along the way, selling carved stones, and bananas among other things. The bathroom shower was a bucket filled with cool water which I poured over my head. I soaped and then poured from the bucket again to rinse. It was October and still monsoon, and on my last afternoon before traveling to the hostel in Auroville, rain fell in a torrent they call elephant rain. By the next morning, I had a terrible cold. Colds seem to purify me and help release emotional baggage that comes up during meditation retreats.

Upon arriving at the guest hostel, I was led to an upstairs room that had expansive windows looking into the trees. It felt like a treehouse. There was a twin bed along the wall, decorated with a few colorful pillows, and down a short hallway was a large, white tiled bathroom with a shower. I felt luxurious, and experienced a deep rest that restored me to health in a few days. Delicious meals were served buffet style and eaten on the patio with other international guests. The next day, a woman from Germany and I toured Auroville and Pondicherry with a knowledgeable, friendly driver. The other few days of my visit,

I explored the area by bicycle. I learned about the community from a movie at the town center. The centerpiece is a gold-plated dome building with garden spokes fanning out circling the dome, each with its own theme and landscape. Tour buses arrive all day long to go inside. I purchased my ticket the day before and joined the long line. Inside the dome, we were given white socks to wear, and were led along a white carpeted walkway circling up to a seating area. We were able to sit quietly for five minutes in the silent energy of the dome, and then were led out to enjoy the gardens. As I remember, the purpose and design of the dome was to increase mental clarity in a seeker. On the outskirts of the dome and gardens stood a massive old Bodhi Tree, which are spiritually significant trees in India.

I learned that when Auroville was opened in the sixties, men and women from all over the world came and brought dirt from their home countries, built a fire and placed the dirt in the flame that is still burning today. Auroville was conceived in a dream by the Mother, a French woman who served Shri Aurobindo in his ashram in Pondicherry, India, and became a revered teacher herself. It is a living, evolving example of people coming together in a world community to help save our planet, to design a new way of collaborative, communal living that honors Mother Earth. Created lovingly from a patch of red dirt surrounding the ancient Bodhi Tree she envisioned in her dream, Auroville is fueled by lofty ideals. On the website, it says, "The purpose of Auroville is to realise human unity—in diversity."

Having dreams and inner visions don't do much for us or society unless we can realize them on the physical plane. Once we've made an internal shift, our perceptions change, and then our behavior changes. We start doing right action, speaking out and standing up for what we care about. Even if the steps are tiny, as long as they are in the right direction, they will eventually lead you where you want to go. It's the combination of all the individuals doing their inner work and taking outer action that will create enough weight to tip the scales back to balance. I do what I can—I recycle trash, I stopped using plastic water bottles and replaced them with my own metal bottle and purifier in a pitcher. I traded my beloved convertible sports car in for a hybrid. What else can I do?

To me it's the everyday small choices we make that make a difference. Shut the water off while you brush your teeth, recycle, turning off the light when you leave a room, walking instead of driving to the next store across the huge parking lot, bringing your own reusable bags to the grocery store. It's the little things done over and over that make a huge difference, by more and more of us who change our behavior and consumption patterns.

The higher the level of self-awareness and consciousness we have, the better we are able to discern fact from fiction, and the more connected we are to our essential core that never dies, the more equipped we are to withstand and stay present to chaos and cataclysmic change. Our souls know the truth with all the devastation in recent years—all-time record setting weather and natural disasters, over and over, now hitting home. It is easy to ignore when it is across the globe, but not so easy when it hits our own front and back yard. The inner work we do to transform ourselves also transforms the world. It is vital, important work, never more so than today when there is so at stake.

This book has been written across several years, and now in 2020, as it is prepared for publishing, the stakes have been raised exponentially, due to the latest coronavirus pandemic which causes the disease COVID-19. The world has been in a rolling lockdown, and life as I knew it no longer exists. Other than the front-line workers, in health care, research and essential business, the best way for the rest of us to contribute to getting this under control is to stay home. I work from home, so it's been an easier adjustment for me. In many ways it has simplified my life, having meetings on Zoom and slowing down. But, it has been devastating on every level—the death toll, economic disaster, isolation from family, friends, social life and freedom of movement. Fear, conspiracy theories, and even denial of the severity are rampant, increasing polarization and nationalism. Staying present, centered in the unchanging, is the only way to discern proper care, protocols, right action in each moment that will keep us, our loved ones and those we lead safe from harm—and alive. Standing in your own truth takes on even greater significance when confronted with crisis and chaos that most of us never dreamed was possible.

It happened virtually overnight. It didn't happen in a vacuum as an isolated incident. It is inextricably tied to climate change, and has been predicted by epidemiologists and climatologists. We have entered a collective global trauma that will last quite some time. If I believed it only as a concept, I am now learning in real time that there is absolutely nothing outside I can control. The only chance I or any of us have is to turn within, and tap into the infinite power that is there, guiding and protecting every move. Complete surrender grants peace in a crumbling world. It also conveys heightened intuition, the ability to listen to and follow inner guidance that enables successful navigation through treacherous waters.

We have returned, albeit temporarily, to a simpler life. In the quietude of quarantine, birds can be heard, the sky is clear blue again, and simple rituals like cooking have time to be appreciated and enjoyed.

This poem was inspired by Alice Walker's poem, "We Have a Beautiful Mother," from collection, *Her Blue Body Everything We Know: Earthling Poems: 1965–1990 Complete.*

Mother Earth, She is Precious

Walking along the lake path,
and a river hidden by yellow leaved trees,
in the cool shadow of hills,
I am calmed.

Listening to crashing waves
against a boulder lined shore,
the ocean spray cooling my face,
I receive solace.

Waking up to birdsong
at first light
opening the blinds,
I am filled with anticipation.

Later, washing zucchini, crookneck squash,
chopping sweet potato and mushrooms
crushing garlic in olive oil and a squeeze of lemon,
I am grateful for sustenance.

Mother, I am forever your child.
You give and give and give.
I take and take and take.
Finally, offering you my bones.

Equal Vision

Another area of society that requires inner soul searching, change, and mass outer action is the civil rights movement. When we know our own intrinsic value, and the truth of our fundamental connection to everything and everyone in the world, that we all share the same divine essence, then we obtain equal vision. Yes!

Before this, it is difficult to have intimate relationships with our self or others. When we carry guilt, shame, and feelings of unworthiness, we hide behind a persona that we think will be more acceptable. The unwanted parts of our self become hidden and shut off. We create distance from others, lest they see through us, as the fakes we are. We begin to project unwanted parts of our self onto others, making them bad or inferior, so we don't have to feel that pain. This happens in families, where members judge and blame each other. Often, one member becomes the scapegoat for the whole family, to mask the behavior of the rest. For instance, the label, black sheep of the family is placed on a member that doesn't perform as expected, gets in trouble, or goes their own way. It's a way for the rest of the members of a dysfunctional system to feel okay about themselves, and lets them off the hook to change themselves and the system.

The family unit is a microcosm of larger groups, and projecting and scapegoating happens at all layers of society. Distinctions are made, differences are focused on, and negative labels are attached. The result is alienation of one person or group by another. The inequality is established, one claims superiority, the other feels the sting of inferiority. The superior think it is their right to exploit, while those judged inferior feel disenfranchised. This is being played out in anti-immigration and separatist movements sweeping Europe and the United States. In the U.S., young children have been separated from parents seeking asylum, neither knowing where the other is or what happened to them. This cruel and inhumane practice will leave permanent scars on these children. It is hard to believe a civil society can behave in this manner. Thankfully, there are those who stand up and march, report and advocate, continuing to keep it in the light.

Inequality also happens innocently, as a result of hierarchies of family, work, and societal structures. One or a few have the responsibility to lead, and the others to follow. We all have different ages, stages in life, knowledge, skill levels and aptitudes that put some in authority and others in subordinate positions. These differences though, do not make us unequal as human beings. It is our flawed perception that makes it appear that way.

Relationships of submission-dominance create a power differential, which can be exploited by those in power for generations. Two glaring examples of this are race and gender. Fortify and expand the differential with the power and influence of government, religion and education, and you can see the reason behind the conflicts that are playing out on the world stage today. People will only put up with feeling inferior and disenfranchised for so long, before they rebel, either violently or peacefully. Conscious leaders, such as Gandhi, Martin Luther King, and Nelson Mandela led peaceful movements for change, but were met with violent opposition. Suffragists and leaders of the women's liberation movement in the United States, such as Gloria Steinem, were peaceful activists for change.

It is horrifying to see incidents of violence and death against African American males by vigilantes and members of the police force around the country. It is also heartening to witness the many acts of solidarity in the demonstrations around the country with participants of many colors protesting the recent deaths at the hands of those sworn to protect.

I am sad to say, even in my extended family there is misunderstanding and hatred by one disturbed son of a family friend who I watched grow up from infancy. As a birthing coach along with his dad, I witnessed his birth and was first to hold him, so I feel a strong bond of love and connection to him. As a grown man, he liked to shock and goad me by texting poems and pictures full of disturbing rhetoric, which I assume he got off the internet. I used think I needed to engage, but I learned painfully that people won't change until they decide it's in their own best interest. Reacting is exactly what he was trying to get me to do, so I didn't respond. After a particularly disturbing text which contained veiled threats to himself and others, I decided to call the police and report what was happening. Keeping silent and/or staying in denial about destructive behavior is a misguided notion to protect that can lead to dire consequences, as we've witnessed too often on the news. It took some soul searching, but the thought of being interviewed on television one day in the aftermath of something horrific saying, "He's such a nice young man. I never thought he could do something like this!" was enough to make me take personal responsibility and report what I knew and feared. I stopped feeling obligated to continue a relationship with someone that holds and expresses a hateful perspective, even as I still love the human being and core of goodness I know is there.

Conscious leadership isn't just on a massive scale, by marching or delivering speeches. Conscious leadership at its most profound is a state of being and a philosophy of life. It is standing in your truth, speaking truth to power, and providing a living example of courage, civility, compassion, and respect for everyone and everything. Conscious leadership is not turning away from something uncomfortable or inconceivable, rather it requires facing hard realities head on and assuming personal responsibility to do what is required in whatever situation you are faced with.

The last thing I wanted to do was report someone I care deeply about to the police. I faced a backlash from his mother, who later came to understand why I had to do what I did. I also experienced fears of retaliation for sometime after, although nothing happened. The fear of his personal safety and the safety of others over rode the fear I felt for myself.

I heard Andrew Harvey, the author of *The Hope: A Guide to Sacred Activism,* speak at an Omega Institute conference some years back, and one thing he said stuck with me, and that is to become a sacred activist for whatever cause you care about. If you love cats or dogs, be an animal rights activist, or volunteer at your local shelter. If you are an avid surfer, join Surfrider Foundation or pick up plastic off the beach. There are endless causes and needs for money, volunteers, and advocacy. Be a foster parent or a Big Brother or Sister. Support Planned Parenthood or join the Women's March. Whatever you are passionate about, just follow your heart and get involved. Most importantly, be informed. VOTE. Stop taking democracy for granted and exercise your right as a free citizen to be heard. With the current wave of authoritarian leaning leaders in the world, our freedom is at risk. Our need to develop more conscious leaders is of paramount importance. Don't give up in despair and disillusionment. Every single vote makes a difference.

It was my first day loose on the tiny town of Madrid, New Mexico, a former mining town on the Turquoise Trail, just outside Santa Fe, where I share a second home with friends and spent some retreat time twice a year. It was Mother's Day, and I was recovering from laryngitis. With my voice still hoarse, I greeted a local named David. With tattoos and leather, he fit well in this eclectic town of rebellious artists, bikers, and healers. We shared a wood bench in the sun, warming ourselves in the chilly springtime air. A few minutes later, as I rose to walk home, he said, "I can tell you about a previous life when you didn't have a voice."

He had my attention. Having been silent for a solid week with laryngitis, I was open, restless, and highly curious. I said "yes" to a double reading and was led inside a little secondhand clothing shop to a table, where his partner, Silvianne Delmars, (featured in the book Nomadland, which was adapted to film and won three academy awards including Best Picture, Actress and Director Oscars in 2021!) did a tarot reading, while David sat outside waiting for my story to further reveal itself to him. He walked in as I was receiving the finishing touches of an uplifting and positive card layout, the message being I had completed a difficult period of transformation, and it was time to go out and shine in the world.

David sat across the antique oak table, and spread open a sheet of white lined notepad paper, filled with handwritten notes. He said, "I was sitting out there on the bench and my pen was flowing, and all of a sudden it stopped, and I couldn't figure out why. Then I realized, your story wasn't finished." He then told me the following story he had written of my past life as a mute, and the journey I was called to make:

You have a Voice

It was a Nordic setting, a time of peace, where there was no need to speak of growth and prosperity. You were restless, feeling a change in the wind. Something was approaching, and you had no voice. It was a change bringing growth, a time to move forward. You knew it was time to change and move, but those around you had become sedentary. No one paid attention to your gestures, your silent screams.

You took it upon yourself to leave, to move, to go forward. You left and left the noise of compliance and contentment behind. You journeyed far and lived off the land. While you ate little, you were never hungry. You were fed by Spirit and heard the voices of Spirit.

Your journey came to a stop in Northern Germany, where you met a kindred spirit in the form of an old gypsy traveler. She took you in and taught you the ways of the traveler, not the ways of the gypsy. She taught you how to write in many tongues, and gave you the voice you never had. You traveled with her for some time and as her time in the physical world came to an end, you honored her by burying her and not cremating her. You laid her in a cave and surrounded her with her most precious things. To this day, she is still there where you left her. She says thank you for honoring her.

You inherited what you did not leave there and journeyed back home. Upon arrival, you found destruction and death. It was validation for you. Without a voice, without a sound, you became a conscious leader. You taught a new way to communicate and to listen. You taught people how to listen to their instinct, because you knew that instinct was the voice of spirit. And so you began a lineage, a heritage of a new way of communication. It filtered through the lands and started communities of art, languages, and appreciation of silence and meditation.

In this life you have a voice.

———

It touched me deeply, because I had just come from a morning walk in the hills surrounding the town, feeling the loss of my mother, expressing my gratitude for her and feeling her there with me on the trail on Mother's Day.

David closed by saying, "Writing is the primary way for you to communicate and make a difference in the world. It is what you need to be doing. It is for you to pick up the pen and finish the story."

As I wrote recounting this story, it was the holiday season, and I was silenced again by laryngitis after Christmas night. The summer before, after a two year writing hiatus, I reinvented my part of the book I spent a year writing with a partner. The partnership had dissolved three months after my mom died, and I became dry as a bone. All creative juices flowed out with my tears, it seemed. Nothing was emerging from the pen. It's clear in retrospect that this is the book I was supposed to write. As painful as the split was, I'm eternally grateful for the lessons, and the spark that was ignited to add prose in addition to poetry to my writing repertoire. To combine them both into the three sections here, the three stages of a journey, came to me that summer as I was creating special coaching packages for my website.

Writing comes in fits and starts. Sometimes it is necessary to lie fallow for the seeds to germinate and produce. Other times life interrupts and demands full attention. The trick is to learn to tell when it is a necessary pause or inertness brought on by doubt. Laryngitis is a gentle reminder to hibernate in silence for a week and see what emerges on the page. When words flow again, give thanks to the darn bug. I'm listening!

It is time for each of us to pick up the pen and write our own story, which becomes the collective story, of how we want life on this planet to be. How do we want to treat our Earth Mother? With the more of the same domination and degradation, or with honor and respect, so that she will remain for many more millennia? We each have been gifted with a unique voice, and it is time to let it be heard.

Action Step:

- Where in your life are you mute?

- If you could speak up about anything, without fear of judgment or retribution, what would it be?

- Speak it, write it, paint it, bring it to the light of day.

- Who has had the biggest influence on you?

- What are you just putting up with?

- Is it a legacy you are grateful for, or is it time to leave it behind?

- What is the change you want to see in the world?

- It's time to embody that change.

- What is the legacy you want to leave?

A fire burns within me in solidarity with women throughout time who have been shackled, abused, and even murdered in the name of patriarchy, as well as for those of us who make it work, paying a price in other ways.

I think this quote by one of my favorite authors, Clara Pinkola Estes introduces the following poems well: "One of the most calming and powerful actions you can do to intervene in a stormy world is to stand up and show your soul. Struggling souls catch light from other souls who are fully lit and willing to show it."

Feminine Uprising

It was I who kidnapped her
and sold her soul for a
few atta boys!
I bought the famous '60's line,
Think like you, talk like you,
fuck like you
and be well compensated for my time.

Be in control.
The A personality thrives.
Production, Business, Money is where it's at.

The left brain carries the real value, you see.
Power and wealth gain respect in this society.
Throw out pagan ways was the battle cry
keep the creative force in her place.
A womb is only a delivery basket
To disdain once the cord is cut.
Yes, I locked her in a dungeon and threw away the key.
Feminine wiles nothing but trouble.
Anger is a source of strength, unless wearing a skirt—
then it's just a ball-busting bitch.
Don't take her seriously, she's crazy.
Weakness is not a virtue, its suicide!

By society's standards, I'm top of the heap.
Buried deep underneath is that dungeon key.
I've started digging recently.
As my body changes with age,
its undergoing a major thaw,
melting carefully crafted image control.

A fire burning from the inside out!
Clearing the fog of skewed perceptions
defining power only one way.
The game not so fun anymore
upon discovery of the real price paid.
The necktie that's strangling me
was tied by my own knot.
Digging through the heap,
I found the key.
Throwing open the dungeon door

letting the brilliant sun shine through.
Loosen the noose and hear the primal scream!
Let the raging waters flow!
Coming into fullness of my body at last,
cherishing every curve and recess
I honor the inner Flame.
The rational and irrational merge in a quantum leap.
Infinite possibilities in a brave new world.

Immanent Power

Hail Mary, welcome home again.
We relegated you to a back wall
So your message would quiet and disappear.
We were heady with success, out to conquer the world.
Who needs motherly admonitions
About brotherly love and peace?

Man over lowly matter.
We name it,
We rule it,
Shape it to fit our needs.
That works on native peoples too.
Why, we can show them a better way.
They understand the cross when shot through the barrel
of a gun.

Hail Mary, make your presence known.
Our corporate veils are thinning,
The King's not wearing any clothes.

The tides are slick with black gold,
Your shimmering moon is shrouded by smoke.
And the earth cries for the voice of balance.
Your rhythms we've forgotten,
Our rituals are dry and stale.
We pray to the almighty Man in the sky
And debase the mother snake coiled in her hole.

Hail Mary, come and shed those virgin robes!
Reveal your divine power
To create and destroy.
We need you now in full glory,
To wield your sword of love
and cut through the muck.

Unobstructed may the Light then shine.
And the earth breathes relief.

Heart's Desire

When I first started in the real estate business, I read about the power of intention, and the importance of having a clear, detailed written statement in order to achieve goals. I wrote my statement, and made a big income goal. I repeated it faithfully every day for years, never giving up hope that one day I would achieve my goal. I came close a few years, and then, finally I reached it! But, I couldn't hold on to what I made or maintain that level of income for a sustained period.

Then I embarked on a path of self-development and began to form a connection to my inner self. I spent many solitary hours bicycle riding and hiking. First, I found a rock by a roadside to sit quietly upon. Then, I wanted to go deeper and find a quieter space. So I left behind my bike and ventured into the canyon I viewed from my original rock. I found another big rock to sit on at the mouth of the canyon. Soon, I wanted to venture deeper, and I followed a trail through a dry creek bed into the heart of the canyon. There was a big, flat rock at the side of the trail, that stretched as long as I was. This became my center, my place of refuge. Here, among wildflowers, lizards and hummingbirds, I learned to listen to my heart, and discern its real desires.

A few years later, feeling at peace within myself, I achieved the biggest volume year of my career. It was far beyond any goal I had ever set. It was a life-changing lesson for me. I realized, without a doubt, the difference was that I was connected to my heart, and I was able to listen and follow my deepest heart's yearnings. The underlying false beliefs about being undeserving were gone. My thoughts, feelings, words, and actions were congruent.

We live in a consumer world where the health of our economy is based upon how much money we spend. This mandates that we create an atmosphere of scarcity and competition, the have's and have-not's. Lynne Twist, who has raised over $300 million for the Hunger Project, in her book, *The Soul of Money*, talks about how giving and service changes our relationship with money, and our definition of prosperity and sufficiency:

> When I made that first contribution to the Hunger Project, it realigned my priorities. My financial life started to be more in alignment with my deep sense of self and soul. I began to have an experience of prosperity that was unrelated to any quantity of money or acquisitions. I could feel this alignment within myself, and I had done that through my use of money. That was the place where the tide turned in me. It was so surprising that money, this very thing I had used and seen others use to perpetuate accumulations, depletion, and making myself important with art and wine and stuff, ended up being *the same instrument* that I eventually used to express my love for people and my affirmation of life, and to share my deepest dreams. Once that instrument, or vehicle called money, was in alignment with my soul, that was when prosperity, joy, and sufficiency started to flourish. It wasn't in the money, but as an instrument of soul.
>
> That is possible for everyone: not only on a personal level, but also on a family level, a cultural level,

society wide. Lining money up with our soul, with our deepest dreams and highest aspirations is the source of our prosperity, rather than simply having more of it to work with. Money used this way connects us to the whole of life, rather than money becoming an instrument that separates and fragments us from each other. That kind of prosperity is available to everyone, whether they are people with massive resources or people with moderate or fewer resources.

Using money as a direct expression of one's deepest self is a powerful, miraculous thing.

For most of my adult life, I've bought into the scarcity, consumer model. I wanted money and affluence, and to look the part. When my former husband and business partner, Bob and I decided to donate a percentage of our income, it gave purpose and meaning to our work. It put giving on the income side of the balance sheet, rather than getting lost among the bills. It was so rewarding to earn a fat commission and write a big check to our favorite foundation. It even transformed the way we felt about paying income taxes. We became grateful to support our community, state, and country through the earning power democracy gives us. We paid our credit cards off every month and became debt free, except for a mortgage on the house.

It was wonderful to give generously and be financially secure. I still loved having nice things, traveling and spending way too much money on restaurant meals, but I didn't go overboard and spent well within our means. I spent too many years in debt and financial insecurity to blow my great good fortune and abundance. I appreciated everything I had and looked to create a stable future. Those high earning years set me up for security in my retirement, as long as I managed finances prudently.

Money is not the goal; it is the instrument that allows me to serve, directly and indirectly, and make a difference in the world. I realized I have a responsibility to prosper to the best of my ability, so that not only do I have sustainability, but everything I touch has the capacity to become sustainable. We have to sustain ourselves in order to be of value to any other person or cause. Lynne Twist writes,

> Every moment of every day there are chances to participate in expressing your individuality and creativity, in contributing to your vision for yourself, your family, your community, city or world. When we bring this consciousness to our choices about money and use our resources—money, time or talents—to take a stand for what we believe in, we come alive. We are flooded with a sense of purpose even in the smallest action, and a feeling of power and energy opens up in your life.

These poems are an exploration of my evolving personal philosophy, as I studied and deepened my understanding of the origin of creativity and manifestation.

Cosmic Answers

Think and Grow Rich—my bible as a young adult.
Faithfully I read aloud as instructed
a daily recitation of my handwritten goal—
the largest income I could possibly conceive.
Year after year, tenaciously repeating,
the goal was finally reached.

I came across an amazing passage while
looking through the ashram library shelf
in a book from 1948, *Devatma Shakti,*
Kundalini Divine, written by an Indian monk:

> *Napoleon Hill, in Think and Grow Rich*
> *says that sexual energy can be transmuted*
> *to higher creative energies of science, art and*
> *poetry...transmutation of sexual energy can easily make one develop*
> *in him or her the "sixth sense,"*
> *inner voice of inspiration and divine communication.*

Having been liberated by women of the sixties,
I ignored Hill's suggestion of sexual sublimation.

> *A yogi does not stop there,*
> *but with full determination, proceeds on*
> *to reach the top of full evolution of self.*

Further along, my mind is blown wider,
when I find my argument as a twelve-year-old
that there can't be a God because
something can't come from nothing—
to say that there is a God!

> *Something cannot come out of nothing,*
> *therefore we are led to believe*
> *that fundamental electronic particles*
> *are formed of some cosmic energy*
> *possessing life...*
> *either reflecting life itself or a form of the life principle.*

Life is created from one's perspective.
It's my heart's intention
to find its way home,
to the vast cosmos within.

I learned from years of daily reading
that old, dry statement
that no desire worth achieving
comes outside the heart.
When it finally arrives
at its destination
all desires slip away.

Meeting the Goddess

You came bursting forth
From my heart.
A light, a power,
An energy
Vibrating through my body.
Tingling softness caressing
The inside of my being
Revealing my soul.

In Search of the Drummer

In the quiet recesses, are new worlds to explore.
I'll take a picnic; be gone awhile.
Keeping a steady pace, I remain aware of each step,
Planting my feet firmly in the soft brown earth.
Greeting wildflowers, lizards, and snakes along the path.

Listening, suddenly, a whirring vibration
stops me, frightened in my tracks.

Investigating, I turn sharply
and see a hummingbird poised in midair,
its glistening purple and vivid green body
held by blurred wings.
Our gazes seemed to meet and hold,
hearts pulsating at the same rate.

I realize then, there's nothing to fear.
We are kin, all of us here.
Beating to just one drum.

Action Step:

Listening to your deepest heart's desires

- What is most important to me right now?

- What am I most passionate about?

- If I could be doing anything I want right now,
  what would it be? Who would I be with?
  Where would I be?

- What impact do I want to have on this world?

- What do I want to be remembered for?

- Does my life reflect my deepest heart's desires?

- Do my interactions with others honor my deepest
  heart's yearnings?

- What are three things I could do right now to make my
  life be more aligned with my heart?

Intimacy: Connecting Heart to Heart

*I*ntimacy is the state of being completely present with what is within our self and outside our self, without judging or trying to change it in any way, attach to it or avoid what is present. It is an open state of authenticity, without posturing or pretense. Intimacy is being in the flow of the moment. To experience true intimacy requires an opening of the heart. It is to be with self or another without masks, taking a risk to expose one's true self. When I let my guard down, and let go of the fear of judgment or rejection, intimacy happens. I can experience deep intimacy within myself, within my soul, the source of Being. Intimacy can happen when two people are sharing something together, a tragic loss, a moving piece of music, or an activity, like a quiet walk. Sometimes there are no words needed, and other times intimacy happens when someone bares their soul, and shares their deepest secrets or yearnings. The love and sacrifice a parent gives to a child is intimacy, overcoming their own fears so their children can have a better life. Childbirth, taking part and witnessing the miracle of life, is one of the most intimate moments to behold.

Intimacy is about being in the present moment, fully focused on the other person, and the feelings arising within one's own heart. Mental chatter has ceased, or is far in the background.

Judgment is suspended, and there is an acceptance of self and other, and the circumstances of the moment. Senses are heightened, as there is full concentration on moment. It can be as if time is suspended.

For many of us, intimacy is elusive. Caught up in the fluctuations of mental chatter, we miss out on what is happening right in front of us, and deep within. The ego is always protecting itself by bolstering its own story and covering up what it perceives as contrary or threatening. It takes vigilance to stay self-aware and continually bring our self back to presence. Connecting to our breath, in a balanced standing posture, and bringing our mind to where our hands are just a few practices to cultivate present moment awareness.

It is not always comfortable to be with what is. Remembering that although we may not have a choice in our circumstances, we have a choice in our attitude and reaction to the circumstance. This is where we gain personal power over our life. The more we fight what is, the less power we have. Acceptance is the second step toward personal power to change our circumstances. The first is self-awareness and the knowledge that everything is temporary. As soon as we change our thoughts, everything else changes too. Maybe not outwardly initially, but a shift in perception changes our attitude, emotions and reactions, therefore the circumstance will inevitably change.

Intimacy isn't just the tender, romantic moments of love between two people. Some of the most intimate moments are solitary—absorbed in a fiery sunset, brought to tears by a moving performance, or merged with the constant repetition of feet running on earth, or bicycle wheels spinning, mile after mile; melting into a baby's soft gaze, burrowing into the fur of a treasured pet, or sinking into the heavy relaxation of deep meditation.

The truth is we are what we seek. What our heart is longing for is already inside us. Intimacy is knowing the truth of our own being and experiencing it in the heart. The Truth is that we are inseparable from Oneness, Source, God; however we name it, we are It in our core. It is our essential nature. Everyone and everything is a form of Oneness. On July 5th, 2012, Dennis Overbye, a writer at *The New York Times* reported that scientists have discovered what one scientist termed the "god particle."

> The subatomic particle, known as Higgs Boson, is the underpinning of a force field that permeates everything in the entire universe. It is now thought that it is what creates mass. It seems to be the glue that holds everything together and connects us all.

When we experience Truth in our heart, barriers melt away—fears, insecurities, and falsehoods flee. What's left is lightness of being. All that is left is love—for self, others. and creation. We then have a fundamental trust that all that is happening is perfect, and a knowing that we have an inherent strength to follow the flow, overcoming obstacles along the way. We then see every challenge and difficult person as an opportunity for personal growth, a circumstance created for our benefit. We become grateful, and let go of resistance.

Until this happens, intimacy remains elusive. We can experience stunning intimate moments that stay with us for a lifetime, but to sustain them seems impossible. We resist being with and accepting what is. Our feelings and our circumstances get judged as good or bad, right or wrong, and we either hold on with attachment or run away feeling aversion. Underlying the judging mind is fear. Our mind gets stuck in past memories that have been triggered or races ahead, projecting into the future. We are no longer in the present, and intimacy is lost.

When we are afraid to be with what is, we sometimes create distractions, in our mind, and our environment. We create a diversion by changing the subject, telling a joke, or calling attention to our self or someone else to distract others and our self from the issue at hand, and from what is happening in the moment.

Sometimes, a little levity or distraction is exactly what is called for to diffuse a tense moment, or spark a new direction in a stagnant meeting. The way to tell if it is used unconsciously as avoidance instead of consciously to inspire a needed shift is to be self-aware and bring our attention to our behavior. Honest self-inquiry is necessary to discern between the two.

Origins of Separation

*T*he need to separate ourselves from others stems from our separation from our essential nature. This causes feelings of unworthiness and deep seated fear. Fear comes very early in our lives, when we forget the Truth of our essential nature, of our connectedness. Awareness of being a separate entity with needs that may not be met can be terrifying. A.A. Almaas, in his book, Facets of Unity, calls this a loss of Basic Trust, and it is universal to all of us in varying degrees, depending on the level of care and nurturing we receive, or as Almaas calls it, the lack of holding in the environment. Even in the most loving environment, there still is the inevitable sense of separation, for it is the forgetting of our divine nature that is the most wounding. It is remembering the truth of who we are that is our life's purpose.

At the core of our being is love. When we connect with the Truth that we are pure love, then fear ceases to exist. This connection to our deepest soul is true intimacy. It is to see our self as we really are and love who we are, including our flaws, our checkered past, our most embarrassing moments, and our shameful family history, without blame or judgment. It is seeing beyond the distorted filters of the ego to our authentic self.

When we experience a healing, and we experience connection with everything, then all moments become intimate. Our relationships flourish, because we are no longer trying to get others to fill the emptiness we felt. We no longer feel the need to change others to meet our needs. We trust our circumstances are perfect, no matter how difficult they may be. Our hearts are filled with gratitude, and our actions with spontaneity. We become virtuous, and trust the flow of life.

We perceive beyond the distorted filters of the ego by honest and regular self inquiry. Self-inquiry is taking the time to unwrap the layers of our stories and discern true motives for our actions. It is listening under the mind's self-talk for true feelings to emerge. For this to be effective, we must develop the ability to step out of ourselves and witness our thoughts and actions from a discrete distance. A part of us then remains an observer of our actions and reactions, and especially our thoughts. For some, this means a daily assessment, to honestly review what we observed in an objective, non-judgmental manner. This requires a quiet time to be set aside, with no distractions.

As we've discussed in earlier chapters, clear space, time, and silence are needed to be able to hear what is in our heart. The truth of our self is revealed there. It is time well spent, listening to our heart for our core values, deepest yearnings, disappointments, and to what most fulfills our soul. It is the path to a joyful life, filled with meaning and purpose.

Intimate Relationships:
Couples in Love

Surrender: Let It Unfold

*T*here is a point when you have to give up when you can't do it on your own. You must surrender. I got to that point in the fall of 2007. My husband, Bob and I had just experienced the best years of our lives, money was pouring in—more than we could've ever imagined. We had just remodeled our home. It was my dream home—had everything that I wanted, except a view. It was built on a desert floor. I had hoped for a hillside lot overlooking the sweeping valley and night lights. It was still a beautiful home. On the outside, we had everything; yet, we were fighting all the time. We called a truce after counseling was a disaster. The truce lasted nine months, and now it was coming to a head again. I stood at my new kitchen sink one evening. All of a sudden, it came over me—fear. I knew he was leaving and it was all coming to an end. I was terrified. I went to my meditation room and bowed at the altar we created. I dropped to my knees— "Please help me. I can't do it on my own. You have to do it for me." I surrendered; all of me.

A few days later we got in a huge fight and decided to separate. I said I wanted to go to India he said no, he wanted to move out. I let it go, and he went house hunting. Everything he looked at did not meet his criteria, finally, he found the perfect place, and a friend of mine he didn't like lived right next door! It was one thing or another, but nothing was acceptable. One night we were sitting in the family room at opposite ends of the sofa, watching TV, and he said how much he would miss his hot tub, pool, and widescreen TV. I said, why don't you let me go to India, and we'll save the rent on another place and not get stuck in a long lease? He paused, and said, "Alright, if you're going to do it do it quick." I applied to the ashram, our separation was completed with an attorney, and we divided our money into separate accounts. I received a visa at the last moment with a trip to San Francisco the weekend before I was leaving, and we got it done.

I flew to India right after Thanksgiving. My life was no longer run by me. I let go of control. I was so devastated that's all I could do. The next four months in India, I let go of everything. My motto became "Let it unfold." Halfway through the stay, I became willing to leave what I held dear. It became clear my life in the desert was finished. I knew if I hung onto that house and stay put in that life, I would go down with the ship. I knew it was time to leave. I had no idea what I was going to do. Let it unfold. I called my mom and asked her if she would like me to live with her. Being in her mid eighties she said she had been so worried about what she was going to do—and she would love me to be with her.

At the same time, I received a letter from my husband that he was moving out and buying another place. I called him quickly and said, "No, you can't go. I don't want the house. I am going to travel for a year and then take care of my mom. You can keep the house."

I hung up, stunned. It was all settled, and I had to catch up with it. Everything was falling in place, with little effort on my part. The enormous challenge was to trust and let it happen as it should. I just kept praying to be shown my next step. That is still my prayer today, as new life constantly unfolds.

Waking Up

What happened in the days turned into years?
We were busy living everyday lives,
dreaming our dreams, shedding some tears;
so wrapped up in myself, I couldn't sense the vibes.

The success we shared masked my deepest fears.
In quiet reflection I explored the archives,
digging into failed relationships, past lives.
Pouring over distant memories, cleansed by tears.

My past comes back haunting after all these years.
Life is a broken record, repeating itself with ever sharper jibes,
pressing me harder and harder to overcome my fears.
Please, let this be the final lesson from those musty archives.

I am through with being sad and angry, drowning in my own tears.
Let us start fresh and new, with or without shared lives.
Figure it out individually; even take a few years.
Separate, detangle, say our goodbyes.

Healing our past, making friends with our tears;
moving freely in open space, getting to know our own vibes.

Breaking old patterns set by the weight of old fears;
waking up, meeting again for the first time,
boundless joy in our lives.

Loving. Heartbreak. Still Love

It seems that marriage becomes more difficult to sustain with each generation. It would not be authentic of me to open this topic with a story of how I'd mastered the art of loving relationship. There are many shipwrecks lining my shoreline of love. I've come to view them not as failures, rather each relationship was an integral and necessary chapter of my personal evolution. Life is temporary, and so are relationships. Perhaps endings are one of the most poignant and intimate parts of being in love. Heartbreak can literally rip us open, and bring us about face to look straight into the mirror under fluorescent light. It's not always flattering, but it's honest. Endings have been flashpoints of major transformation in my life.

A heart-to-heart connection is what creates an intimate relationship. There are many marriages created or sustained for reasons other than love, such as financial security, or sustaining a family, and these can resemble business arrangements more than a loving marriage. Love and intimacy can grow from these arrangements, if there is a commitment to one another, and mutual trust is developed.

John O'Donohue, in his book, Anam Cara: *A Book of Celtic Wisdom*, expressed the intimacy between lovers beautifully,

> "When you love, you open your life to an Other. All your barriers are down. Your protective distances collapse.

This person is given absolute permission to come into the deepest temple of your spirit...It takes great courage to let someone so close."

Researchers are finding that emotional connection is what counts in relationships. We have a need for emotional bonding for our health, well-being and very survival. According to Dr. Sue Johnson, a Canadian couples-therapist, a British researcher named John Bowlby did extensive studies and came up with Attachment Theory. In her book, *Hold Me Tight*, she wrote about his findings:

> Love is the best survival mechanism there is, and to feel suddenly emotionally cut off from a partner, disconnected, is terrifying. We have to reconnect, to speak our needs in a way that moves our partner to respond. This longing for emotional connection with those nearest us is the emotional priority overshadowing even the drive for food or sex. The drama of love is all about this hunger for safe emotional connection, a survival imperative we experience from the cradle to the grave. Loving connection is the only safety Nature ever offers us."

Loving connection between two people can grow into an intimate relationship most readily when there is a commitment to be there for one another as monogamous partners. This provides a safe atmosphere where trust is built over time by the supportive, loving actions and behavior of the partners. It is exclusive, and special. Each partner can grow and thrive inside and outside the relationship when nurturing support is given and received. Dr. Johnson continues,

> "If you know your loved one is there and will come when you call, you are more confident of your worth, your value.

And the world is less intimidating when you have another
to count on and you know you are not alone."

It all starts with recognizing that the love we have inside
is our intrinsic nature. Love emanates from within us; it does
not come from an outside source, as most of us believe. When
we connect with the love in our heart, we find it is an endless
source. The more we give love, the more it grows inside us.
It contracts only when we try to hold onto it. It is like the
exchange of breath. If we hold onto it too long, we will pass
out. It is only when we release it that we are replenished with
fresh breath. Unlike breathing, which is automatic and eventually
forces us to release and take a breath, we can hold on tight and
covet love, and it will stagnate and die. Love is longing to be
shared. Like the breath, love will not be contained. It is bursting
inside us to be released and shared. Matching the rhythms of our
breath with our loved one's breath, synchronizes heart rhythms
and emotional states. It is a profound way to share intimacy with
another, to show them you are listening and you care.

If we are connected with our essential loving nature, we
are replenished with love from the inside. There is no longer
a desperate need to seek it outside from some sort of compulsive
stimulation like overeating or drugs, or from the wrong kind
of people. We can discern the difference between a healthy
and unhealthy relationship. We stop projecting shadow parts
of our self onto the other, and see them for who they really
are. We become the love we want. Then it is about offering
and sharing the love we already have. Our cup runneth over.
Some people who obtain this level of self-awareness and self-
love, no longer have a desire to be part of a love partnership.
Their love instead becomes universal. They feel and share love

with everyone, and life becomes service to the uplifting of humanity and the world. Other people can be dedicated to service and still want to grow within the context of a loving, committed relationship.

For me, I choose to be in relationship. I've slowly let go of the fairy tale version of a knight in shining armor that is gorgeous, and witty and committed to love me forever. Instead, my heart wants kindness and ease, truthfulness, and companionship. Shared values and integrity, compassion, and steadfastness. In short, I thrive in a relationship that embodies the virtues.

I have let go of an agenda, a place to get to called marriage. An old version of me thought that was the ultimate way to go, but now I'm not so sure. I'm content with not knowing what the future holds, and I see that marriage holds no guarantees. I practice presence, without trying to direct it in any way, and that is refreshing! My idea of intimacy is changing too. I experience that words aren't everything, and actions speak louder than words. A shallow, *I love you*, pales next to steadfast presence through thick and thin, sickness and health. A quiet acceptance for past and present, without disclosing every last detail, builds trust in a way that may be more powerful than baring all. John O'Donohue, in his book, *Anam Cara: A Book of Celtic Wisdom* said,

> Real intimacy is sacred. It never exposes its secret trust and belonging to the voyeuristic eye of a neon culture. Real intimacy is of the soul, and the soul is reserved.

The poem *Naked Truth* shows that the path to intimacy is traversed from the inside out. When projections are dropped, it is like meeting someone for the first time.

Naked Truth

Fear runs deep, this old belief,
That you matter more than me.
I fear to tell the truth
Would annihilate you.

So stuff the self expression
and be strong,
Sublimating my needs for yours.
What a lie was propagated,
Victim pretending victory.
The illusion a meager reward;
The price—disrespect for us both.

Disrobing that snug cloak
Of superiority,
Raw grace stands naked before you.

Standing here as I am
Unashamed
I look at you for the first time
Seeing your glory.

A Shared Path to Wholeness

*H*arville Hendrix, in his book, *Getting the Love You Want: A Guide For Couples,* describes one of the characteristics of a conscious relationship as follows:

> You become more aware of your drive to be loving and whole and united with the universe. As part of your God given nature, you have the ability to love unconditionally and to experience unity with the world around you. Social conditioning and imperfect parenting made you lose touch with these qualities. In a conscious relationship, you begin to rediscover your original value.

One area of growth that a loving partnership offers is that of healing our past. Another characteristic of a conscious relationship, described by Dr. Hendrix, is,

> You realize that your love relationship has a hidden purpose—the healing of childhood wounds. Instead of focusing entirely on the surface needs and desires, you learn to recognize the unresolved childhood issues that underlie them. When you look at relationships with this X-ray vision, your daily interactions take on more meaning. Puzzling aspects of your relationship begin to make sense to you, and you have a greater sense of control.

When we are by ourselves, it is easy to imagine that we are secure, and free from the wounds of our childhood and past relationships. When there is no one rubbing close against us to trigger uncomfortable memories and emotions, we can be deluded into thinking we have it all together! Why are we resistant or afraid to enter into a new relationship? Why do we sabotage any chance of it happening by overworking, isolating, or acting out compulsive behavior? It is scary to have our flaws exposed and to risk painful memories resurfacing. Yet, the only way to heal ourselves is to try again, in a new way, perhaps with a different type of person. Bottom line is that others are our mirror. We are only as healthy as the person we are attracted to is reflecting back to us. This is what offers the opportunity to heal, if we are willing to look honestly at ourselves, rather than just refracting blame and responsibility onto our partner.

We must tread tenderly though. Awareness that the wound is there may be all that is needed. John O'Donohue, in his book, *Anam Cara: A Book of Celtic Wisdom* goes further and explains why prodding may deepen the wound:

> When you love someone that is very hurt, one of the worst things you can do is directly address the hurt and make an issue out of it. A strange dynamic comes alive in the soul if you make something into an issue. It becomes a habit and keeps recurring in a pattern. Frequently, it is better to acknowledge that the wound is there, but then stay away from it.

It is challenging, because each partner brings their own wounding, personality and way of seeing the world to the relationship, and in many ways these can be complementary or polar opposite to what the other partner brings. We also project hidden parts of our self onto our partner, both disowned and desired traits. Partners have different needs, and express those needs in different ways.

Dr. Sue Johnson says:

> Gender plays a part here, though the roles vary with culture and couple. In our society, women tend to be the caretakers of relationships. They usually pick up on the distance sooner than their lovers and they are often most in touch with their attachment needs. So their role in the dance is most often the pursuing, more blaming spouse. Men, on the other hand, have been taught to suppress emotional responses and needs, and also be problem solvers, which sets them up in the withdrawn role.

As we discussed in the topic of perception in Chapter Two, we each have a unique way of seeing the world. We often erroneously believe that others must see things the same way we do, because it is the right way. This is especially prevalent in couples. We also erroneously believe that our partner can see what we want and need, and selfishly chooses not to respond. Self-responsibility is being able to articulate our needs to our self and others and ask for want we want. It is also the ability to be self-sufficient and meet our own needs where possible. Having expectations of others is what leads to misery, for we are bound to be disappointed, especially when expectations are unrealistic.

Part of becoming self-aware, in addition to seeing that our vision is often distorted, is to realize that others have very different ways of viewing the world, that are equally as valid, as well as sometimes as distorted as ours. It is difficult to experience intimacy with another when we are unaware that we are not experiencing the same thing. The path to healing ourselves and experiencing greater intimacy with another is to care enough about what they think and feel to ask, and then listen openly to what they say, with a true desire to understand their point of view. As long as we are stuck on being right, and not willing to change, chances of healing and intimacy are rare. We are often stubbornly vested in our opinions and viewpoints, because they bolster the importance of our ego, and to change threatens our self-worth. Harville Hendrix, in *Getting the Love You Want, A Guide For Couples*, said,

> Relationships give you the opportunity to be continually schooled in your own reality and in the reality of another person. Every one of your interactions contains a grain of truth, a sliver of insight, a glimpse into your hiddeness and your wholeness. As you add to your growing fund of knowledge, you are creating reality love, a love based on the emerging truth, not on romantic illusion.

According to Dr. Hendrix, there are three steps in effective communication between couples that allow greater connection and bonding in the relationship, that facilitate bridging differences in perception and expression, including those caused by gender:

> When couples master the three-step process of mirroring, validation and empathy, these gender differences begin to diminish. A man, who is emotionally repressed, starts to value empathy as much as his female partner. The reason this occurs is that seeing and acknowledging his partner's feelings makes him more comfortable with his own. Meanwhile, a woman who is emotionally volatile can become less so. Because she no longer needs to amplify her feelings in order to have her stoic partner acknowledge them, she can express them with less force.

When we truly care what our partner feels, thinks, and believes, and can clearly see and respect their point of view, even if it disagrees with ours, we open ourselves to greater intimacy and fulfilling relationships. Although the rewards are great, it isn't always easy to listen, especially when our partner is upset with us, or when they are triggering a childhood wound. It's even harder to mirror and validate what they've said. This is where self-awareness pays off. When we can witness our self becoming upset by what our partner is sharing, we can pause and determine what button is getting pushed and what feeling is underlying the irritation or anger, such as hurt, sadness, or fear. We can then respond in a more responsible, conscious way.

In my current relationship, I am often challenged. My partner and I are of different political affiliations, and frequently have opposing viewpoints. Most of the time, we just agree to disagree, and stay away from controversial subjects. But, sometimes, I just have to express my frustration at current events! I know that I'm not going to change his mind, but I just need to vent and unload. Most of the time I do it while we are on a walk. He gets frustrated, asking if I have to ruin another walk, but he listens without arguing his point. It is more important to be heard than to be right, and I so appreciate that he can just hold space for me without it turning into an argument. When he does share his point of view, I try to be curious and see the deeper perspective.

This is hard to do when I'm caught in the emotional heat of the moment. I definitely can improve in that area. What's really important to remember is that we share the same values. I think that is the case more times than we think. If we can truly listen to another and uncover a shared value system, that is the bridge that can create a common solution. That has become a lost art that needs to be revived in our public discourse, as well as private conversations.

I heard a story recently about a man hiking in the mountainside who thought someone was taunting him as he was yelling to himself. He didn't realize it was his own echo that was disturbing his peace. It brought my attention to my behavior on these walks. When I get caught up in negative emotions, I lose the present moment. The beauty of my surroundings fades into the background, and I might as well be staring at a wall. As I ignore the sky and landscape, I become more and more disillusioned until I catch myself and enforce quiet. As I breathe more deeply and look around again, calmness slowly returns. The story inspired me to promise myself not to ruin another walk!

Dr. Sue Johnson said, "No one can dance with a partner and not touch some raw spots. We must know what these raw spots are and be able to speak about them in a way that pulls our partner closer to us." The safer the container of committed relationship feels by the strength of the commitment, the closer we feel to our partner, and the freer we are to communicate our deepest hurts honestly and openly, trusting we will not be rejected or hurt more. This is heart-to-heart communication at the deepest level. It is where we are most vulnerable. The person we love most and have committed to holds our heart, in essence. The more we feel love and acceptance, the more we can open and allow ourselves to be vulnerable. "The real concern is always the strength and security of the emotional bond you have with your partner. It is about accessibility, responsiveness and emotional engagement," according to Dr. Johnson. If any of those are lacking, the strength and security of the relationship is compromised, and the level of open communication diminishes. If accessibility, responsiveness and emotional engagement are present, intimacy flourishes.

It's All Love

During my third ashram stay in India in 2010, I was sitting on the patio in the dark silence of pre-dawn, sipping chai before the morning devotional chant. The sweet, exotic smell of Queen of the Night blooms permeated the air. I was awash in bliss, and an overwhelming feeling of love came over me. This love wasn't tied to any thought, memory, person, or experience. It was all pervasive, Universal Love, and it was coming from my heart. I did nothing to create it; the love just appeared and took me over.

I chanted and wandered the gardens, praying that this love inside would last and wondering how I could call it back if it didn't. After several hours, I realized it was gone and that holding on to it would be like trying to capture a beautiful sunset and make it stay. To me one of the great things about a spiritual meditation path is to receive these glimpses of the divine, which is a gift of the divine energy that is so present and alive in the ashram.

After that morning of pure love, in the remaining days of my stay, it was if I was looking in a mirror telling myself, "I Love You" over and over—the ashram was reflecting back to me the love I felt inside. I was showered with love. I spent three days cleaning statues in one of the gardens with care and devotion.

I felt as though I was going through purification and initiation. As I washed the feet of one of the saints, I imagined that I was Mary Magdalene, anointing Jesus' feet with precious oil, and that I was being loved unconditionally, as Jesus loved her. It was a gift of healing that will always remain with me.

One late afternoon, hot and sweaty after scrubbing shutters black with mildew from the monsoon, I stopped in the silent courtyard, and filled with overwhelming gratitude, I bowed before the picture of the spiritual master who founded the ashram, touching my forehead to the floor. I remained there, feeling love rush over me. When I raised my head and stood, turning to leave, I glanced at a man entering the courtyard. He gave me the sweetest smile, and his liquid brown eyes melted me. It was a cherished moment of shared love, even though I didn't know who he was.

I was glowing as I walked away, and I wanted to meet him. He was Indian, and I wondered if he spoke English. The following evening, after dinner, I walked out to the grass field on the ashram grounds to watch the sunset. It was a balmy evening, and the damp grass felt cool on my feet. As the orange orb blazed and painted the sky, I looked around and saw him walking on the perimeter path, lined with Peepal trees, which have heart shaped leaves.

I stood quietly in the middle of the field, watching the elegant white cattle egrets swoop in and play in the grass. As he came around the bend, into an open area, I made my way to the path, entering about fifty feet in front of him. Not looking at him, I walked slowly, so he could catch up if he wanted to. Shortly, he was beside me saying hello. He spoke English fairly well, with a heavy accent that was hard to understand. We walked and chatted, and soon I drifted to his side of the path. I thought I heard, "please move," but that couldn't be right, could it? Once again, he spoke under his breath; I still thought I was mistaken. A third time, he spoke louder, "Please move away. In Indian culture, men and women do not walk close unless they are married." I quickly moved to my side of the path, and made sure to stay there!

We continued around twice, laughing and talking. I listened to him share a few Indian legends that have a message about right conduct and action. We sat on a bench for a while, over-looking the beautiful twilight scene. The shared appreciation for the nature we beheld, the love of God and our spiritual path, brought back my earlier experience of Universal Love.

Despite cultural, language, and physical barriers, we opened our hearts to one another. It was one of the sweetest, most intimate moments I've shared with a man. A week later, as I was leaving for the airport for the long flight home, a small group gathered to send me off. A woman asked what the most significant thing was that I learned during my stay. Immediately, it came to me—It's All Love, and it comes from inside of me.

In the years since, I remember my time of retreat, solitude, transition, and friendship, with love and gratitude. There has been great loss, struggles, challenges, and adventure. It has all been colored with the underlying knowledge that it is all about love. When I forget, I breathe into the memories of the ashram gardens, smelling the fragrance of night blooming jasmine and the blossoming of true Love within my own heart.

The love of self and the love for another brings change to the world. Bringing presence and love changes the atmosphere around us and ripples out, for we are all connected. If that is all you offer to the world, it is an enormous gift. It is also a gift to yourself. Put your feet on the earth, lean your body against a tree. Come into resonance with the rhythms of the universe. Listen and be guided by a deep knowing.

Emergence

I was directed down a different path
on a hike one day.
Something inside said, this way.
I listened, and I went.

On a hike one day,
for the first time, I saw the other side of the ridge.
I listened and I went
deep into a place I'd never traversed.

For the first time, I saw the other side of the ridge.
I was led to a rock where I was drawn to lie.
Deep into a place I'd never traversed,
feeling ecstasy against hot granite.

I was led to a rock where I was drawn to lie,
when the sky rammed into me.
Feeling ecstasy against hard granite,
merging with raw elements.

When the sky rammed into me,
colliding forces exploded.
I emerged a woman of the earth, eternally changed;
directed down a different path.

Epilogue

May your heart overflow with Love, may you have peace of mind, and may your life reflect back the infinite beauty that is uniquely you. May you share yourself freely and abundantly, shining brightly as a night star.

It has been a great honor to share my journey and have it be witnessed by you. It is my heartfelt wish that you have been touched and transformed in ways you may or may not know. and that we together are transforming the world.

With Love and Blessings,

S'Marie

Acknowledgments

So many people contributed to this book, directly and indirectly through our shared experiences.

I am eternally grateful to my mom, Beryle for the four years we spent together at the end of her life. We provided a safe haven for one other and often expressed mutual appreciation for that. I came to understand her in a different way, to respond and be healed by her quiet and reserved flavor of love. Those years with her gave me a resting place to reflect, let go, birth a new life, and became the backbone of this book.

Kudos to Beth Fountain, book and cover designer and artist extraordinaire, and so much more—fellow seeker, friend, and the steady presence that saw me as a writer with perspective of great value. Her keen observations helped me to keep going when I had doubts, and to believe in my insights and writing ability.

Thanks to Jennifer Hager, developmental book editor for tearing the book apart and then coming back to validate the three parts that emerged from the ashes of the former collaboration. Cheers to my writing coach, Dawn Montefusco. You sanded, polished, probed, and cajoled, drawing me out, and took me deeper within to get to the vulnerable place, the heart that the book demanded. You also loved my poetry, even encouraging new pieces to emerge. When I was afraid there was too much of me, you demanded more. A third set of exceptional eyes belong to professor and writing coach Kathy Sparrow, who edited the final draft of the manuscript.

Gratitude for Jana Beaman, marketing and master mind coach, for her quick eye and wordsmithing; and Liana Beckett, former publishing house editor and encouraging friend, for our stimulating idea exchanges and her help with quoted work and citations. We are simpatico!

In his forward, James Melton, PhD succinctly expressed the essence of Emergence, elucidating for the reader the benefit of reading further. An author of many books on leadership, and a professional speaker for conferences and corporate gatherings, Jim has always been a thought leader and forward thinker. Jim and wife Dana have been dear friends for twenty-five years; sharing a love of the desert.

At our first meeting, we attended the launch of a weekly symposium hosted by Bill Edelen at The Palm Springs Tennis Club. Every Sunday morning for a few years on, Bill widened my horizons with talks infused with teachings from these books, among others: *Carl Jung, Man and his Symbols; Joseph Cambell, The Power of Myth; Frank Waters, Mountain Dialogs and The Woman at Otawi Crossing; Merlin Stone, When God Was a Woman.* Edelen was a philosopher with strong, unconventional viewpoints. His strongly vocalized anger against Christianity forced me to confront my own. A few years later, I met my meditation teacher, and my heart opened wide with spiritual initiation. After that, as I listened to Bill, his anger felt piercing, as if it was a mirror—exposing, dislodging and releasing my own anger and religious bias. Although I lost interest in listening to

Bill's commentary, Dana, Jim and I continued to have probing conversations about the meaning and purpose of life.

Another lasting friendship formed in those years with Barbara Amita. I was with her and a group of friends when we attended the opening talk and New Year's Day events at a meditation retreat held at the Palm Springs Convention Center in 1995/96. It was there that I received spontaneous spiritual initiation. Amita was a long-time meditator and seeker who connected with other locals at the retreat and formed a fledgling meditation group, which eventually became an official meditation center. She lived with me awhile during that time and would bring me flowers and chocolate after satsang. Eventually, I started attending too. Just feed me chocolate, and I'll go anywhere! Amita was an early panelist for Helen Palmer's Enneagram type panels, and an avid student of the Enneagram. She gave a workshop to a small group and I was hooked. In the years since, Amita has been a spiritual and Enneagram mentor, sister, business partner and closest friend. An intuitive and spiritual teacher in her own right, her insights about me have opened portals to breakthroughs in lasting transformation.

When a major chapter of my life closed at the end of 2007, my next chapter was hand delivered by destiny, and executive coach Jeaneen Schmidt. I first met her when we shared ride to an ashram for a meditation retreat, after arriving in Mumbai on the same plane from LAX. We became fast friends as roommates during the retreat. When we were "accidental" roommates on retreats twice more during 2008, I took it as a sign pointing towards coaching as my next career. Jeaneen referred me to CTI (Coaches Training Institute, now Co-Active Training Institute), where she is one of the leaders for aspiring coaches. She coached me through my biggest life transition and helped me launch my coaching practice. Jeaneen is an exceptional role model, coach and friend.

I am proud to be a Co-Active coach and part of the global community. Two of my most memorable teachers at CTI are Cynthia Loy Darst and David Darst. I will never forget David marching me in and standing behind my tear streaked face in the women's bathroom outside the training room in Pasadena, California, forcing me to acknowledge my inner strength. He was perceptive enough to see beyond my bright demeanor, a heartbroken woman crushed in the throes of divorce.

After studying and using the Enneagram for so many years in my own personal development, I was excited to share what I'd learned with my coaching clients. Ginger Lapid Bogda, PhD showed me how, and provided excellent learning tools through her certification programs for coaching, facilitating and consulting with the Enneagram. At my first training in 2010 in Santa Fe, New Mexico, I met Ginger, and co-facilitator Bea Chestnut, PhD (on Enneagram subtypes) as well as members of the Enneagram community like Ken Sergi and Gerry Fathauer. A few years later, I spent a memorable weekend learning how to deepen relationships using the Enneagram, from premier teachers David Daniels, MD and Russ Hudson.

In addition to being an accomplished coach and Enneagram facilitator, Ken Sergi is an outstanding photographer. He captured the portrait images for the book backcover and my website.

Surprisingly (or not), poetry makes a very significant appearance in this book. I want to thank poet and mentor,

Acknowledgments

David St. John, Idyllwild Arts Poetry Week, and Mifawny Kaiser at Tebot Bach, poetry workshop host, for all the camaraderie with the Los Angeles poetry community, shared work, creative feedback and exposure to great artists and lovers of poetry. Thank you!

Deepest gratitude to these people I have mentioned, and to those I haven't named that are very special; my partner of six years, my spiritual community and loving friends. Your steady presence and encouragement helped me to persevere through loss, grief, health crisis and recovery to keep writing and finish the book.

About S'Marie Young

S'Marie Young has been a lifelong seeker of the truth within. She is a meditator committed to personal development and fascinated with the story behind the story of her own and other's behaviors. Her quest has taken her to India five different times for study and contemplation. An urban yogi that is planted firmly in the world, S'Marie blends her practical business acumen with timeless spiritual principals she has learned, putting them into practice in her own life and sharing her experience with others. She was a sales leader during a twenty-five-year career in commercial real estate, as co-founder of a boutique brokerage firm that was eventually acquired by a company with global affiliations. She served her last six years in the industry working for them as a Senior Vice President. Searching for a career that served the whole person, inside and out, personally, and professionally, she found leadership coaching a perfect fit. As a poet, she is a keen observer, offering creative insights and guidance to clients in a way that penetrates beyond the head and reaches the heart—the place where meaningful change happens. In her leisure time, S'Marie enjoys reading novels, writing poetry, reveling in beautiful coastal and southwest landscapes taking long walks and hikes.

Certifications include: CPCC, Certified Professional Co-Active Coach, with Co-Active Training Institute; Enneagram Prison Project Facilitation; The Enneagram in Business: Coaching with the Enneagram, Enneagram Leadership Facilitation, Consulting with the Enneagram

Resources

Almaas, A.A. *Facets of Unity: The Enneagram of Holy Ideas*. Boston: Shambhala Publications, Inc., 1998.

Bennett-Goleman, Tera. *Emotional Alchemy: How the Mind Can Heal the Heart*. New York: Three Rivers Press, 2001.

Cuddy, Amy. "Your Body Language Shapes Who You Are." Filmed June 2012, at TED Ed, Edinburgh, Scotland. Video, 21:02. https://www.youtube.com/watch?v=RWZluriQUzE

Daniels, David and Suzanne Dion. *The Enneagram, Relationships and Intimacy: Understanding One Another Leads to Loving Better and Living More Fully*. California: KDP Publishing, 2018.

Daniels, David and Virginia Price. *The Essential Enneagram: The Definitive Personality Test and Self-Discovery Guide*. New York: Harper Collins, 2009.

Davis, John V. *The Diamond Approach: An Introduction to the teachings of A.H. Almaas*. Boston: Shambhala Publications, Inc., 1999.

Estés, Clarissa Pinkola. *Let Your Soul Light Shine Bright*. 1/11/2012. https://high-road-artist.com/9189/wisdom-wednesdays/clarissa-pinkola-estes-let-your-soul-light-shine/.(Jeane George Weigel).

Estés, Clarissa Pinkola. *Women Who Run With the Wolves: Myths and Stories of the Wild Woman Archetype*. New York: Ballantine Books, 1992. page 511

Estés, Clarissa Pinkola. *Untie the Strong Woman: Blessed Mother's Immaculate Love for the Wild Soul.* United States: Sounds True, 2013.

Frankl, Viktor. *Viktor Frankl, Man's Search for Meaning.* Boston: Beacon, 2000, 66

Frings Keyes, Margaret. *Out of the Shadows: Uses of Depression, Anxiety, and Anger in the Enneagram.* Muir Beach, CA: Molysdatur Publications, 1988.

Gibran, Kahlil. *The Prophet.* New York: Alfred A. Knopf, 1923.

Harvey, Andrew. *The Hope: A Guide to Sacred Activism.* Carlsbad, CA: Hay House, 2009.

Hendrix, Harville. *Getting the Love You Want, A Guide For Couples.* New York: Henry Holt and company, LLC, 1988.

Huffington, Arianna. *The Fourth Instinct: The Call of the Soul.* New York: Simon and Schuster, 1994.

Huffington, Arianna. *Thrive, The Third Metric to Redefining Success and Creating a Life of Well Being, Wisdom and Wonder.* New York: Harmony Books, Excerpted in Mindful Magazine, taking time for what matters. June, 2014, mindful.org p. 37

Johnson, Dr. Sue. *Hold Me Tight: Seven Conversations for a Lifetime of Love.* New York: Little, Brown and Company Hatchette Book Group, 2008.

Kornfield, Jack. *A Path With Heart: a Guide Through the Perils and Promises of Spiritual Life.* New York: Bantam Books,1993.

Lapid-Bodga, Ginger. *What Type of Leader Are You? Using the Enneagram System to Identify and Grow Your Leadership Strengths and Achieve Maximum Success.* New York: McGraw-Hill, 2007.

Levine, Stephen and Ondrea. *Embracing the Beloved: Relationship as a Path to Awakening.* New York: First Anchor Books Edition, a division of Random House, 1996.

Maitri, Sandra. *The Spiritual Dimension of the Enneagram: Nine Faces of the Soul.* New York: Jeremy P. Tarcher/Penguin, 2001.

Muir, John. *John of the Mountains: The Unpublished Journals of John Muir.* Maison, WI: Wisconsin: The University of Wisconsin Press, 1938. (Edited by Linnie Marsh Wolfe).

O'Donahue, John. *Anam Cara: A Book of Celtic Wisdom.* New York: HarperCollins Publishers Inc, 1998.

Proust, Marcel. *'La Prisonnière', the fifth volume of 'Remembrance of Things Past' (also known as) 'In Search of Lost Time'* http://www.age-of-the-sage.org/quotations/proust_having_seeing_with_new_eyes.html

Rilke, Maria. From *"The Sonnets of Orpheus"* in *The Selected Poetry of Maria Rilke.* New York: Random House, Inc., 1982. (Mitchell, Stephen)

Riso, Don Richard and Russ Hudson. *The Wisdom of the Enneagram: the Complete Guide to Psychological and Spiritual Growth for the Nine Personality Types.* New York: Bantam Books, 1999

Riso, Don Richard and Russ Hudson. *Understanding the Enneagram: The Practical Guide to Personality Types.* New York: Houghton Mifflin Company, 2000.

Rumi, Jalalhuddin, Barks, Coleman, Translator, Green, Michael, Illuminations. *The Illuminated Rumi.* New York: Harmony, 1997.

Simeona, Morrnah Nalamaku. Morrnah Nalamaku Simeona, Hawaiian healer. https://amazingwomeninhistory.com/morrnah-nalamaku-simeona-hawaiian-healer/ (Sita Khalsa)

Shantananda, Swami. *The Splendor of Recognition.* South Fallsburg, New York: SYDA Foundation, 2003.

Tharp, Twyla. Choreographer Twyla Tharp Talks Dancing, Aging, Stirs the Pot. Interview on NPR Podcast: Bullseye With Jesse Thorn. January 17, 2020 npr.org/2020/01/15/796855816/choreo-grapher-twyla-tharp-talks-dancing-aging-stirs-the-pot

(The Mother), Mirra Alfassa. *http://www.auroville.org/contents/526.* Auroville, Tamil Nadu India: Auroville Foundation, 2004.

Twist, Lynne. *Soul of Money: Transforming Your Relationship With Love and Life.* New York: W. W. Norton & Company, 2006.

Walker, Alice. *The Curtain in the Road: Meditation and Wandering as the Whole World Awakens to Being in Harm's Way.* New York: The New Press, 2013

Whitworth, Laura, Karen Kimsey-House, Henry Kimsey-House and Phillip Sandahl. *Co-Active Coaching: New Skills for Coaching People Toward Success in Work and Life.* Mountain View California: Davies Black Publishing, 2007

CPSIA information can be obtained
at www.ICGtesting.com
Printed in the USA
LVHW011250230721
693278LV00008B/334